HOW TO

COLLECT
CHILD SUPPORT

HOW TO

COLLECT
CHILD SUPPORT

GERALDINE JENSEN
KATINA Z. JONES

LONGMEADOW PRESS

Published by Longmeadow Press, 201 High Ridge Road, Stamford, CT
06904. All rights reserved. No part of this book may be reproduced or
utilized in any form or by any means, electronic or mechanical, including
photocopying, recording or by any information storage and retrieval
system, without permission in writing from the Publisher.

Cover design by Dorothy Wachtenheim
Interior design by Hannah Lerner

Library of Congress Cataloging-in-Publication Data

Jensen, Geraldine.
    How to collect child support / Geraldine Jensen and Katina Jones.
— 1st ed.
        p. cm.
    ISBN 0-681-41185-6
    1. Child support—Law and legislation—United States—Popular
works. I. Jones, Katina. II. Title.
KF549.Z9J46   1991
346.7301'72—dc20
[347.306172]   91-32754
                                                                   CIP

ISBN: 0-681-41185-6

Printed in *United States of America*

0 9 8 7 6 5 4 3

For who it's all about—Matt & Jake.
                              —G.J.

For A.Z., H.Z. and Louis.
                    —K.Z.J.

CONTENTS

PREFACE

The contents of this book are based on legal information provided to the Association For Children For Enforcement Of Support (ACES) by attorneys from Advocates For Basic Legal Equality (ABLE). *How To Collect Child Support* is not intended to provide legal advice. You should contact an attorney for legal advice if you feel it would benefit your case. Please note that the Federal Child Support Program has an office in each state which is required to provide an attorney for child support enforcement and establishment cases, if needed, at a maximum $25 fee.

Introduction

AFTER HER 1977 divorce, Geraldine Jensen returned to Toledo from Omaha, Nebraska with her two young sons, Matthew, 4, and Jake, 18 months. For six months, her former husband paid child support but then it abruptly stopped. Unable to make enough money to support her family as a library aide, she was forced to go on welfare.

Bolstered by two federal grants from Pell and Title XX, Gerri returned to school in 1980, and a year later graduated from Bowling Green School of Practical Nursing. As a licensed practical nurse, she was hired to supervise other LPNs at a nursing home.

Though struggling, she was making it until the end of 1983—when everything caved in. Stricken with an illness that put her in intensive care, she was hospitalized for three weeks. In addition, her son needed ear surgery to prevent hearing loss.

With no money or savings, she telephoned her caseworker of seven years at the County Welfare Department to inquire about $12,000 due to her in back support. Informed that the County Prosecutor's office had actually been handling the case, a bewildered and stunned Gerri confronted the prosecutor.

With her case file in front of him, he told Gerri that nothing could be done about the child support collection. "If you can do a better job, then go right ahead," he said.

Geraldine Jensen did exactly that. She spent eight of her last $12 on a classified ad in the Sunday *Toledo Blade,* an act which changed her life forever.

The ad read, "Not receiving your child support? Call me."

Little did Gerri realize the effect this ad would have on Toledo women. Ten women responded by that Sunday evening. Within two weeks, the Association For Children For Enforcement Of Support (ACES) was formed—with 50 women as members. Two months later, the group ballooned to 200.

FAMILIES AFFECTED BY DIVORCE

American Statistic: One-half (50%) of all American families divorce.

Robin and Larry were married in 1980. This was six months after they graduated from high school. They set out to live the American Dream. Larry worked full time at the local factory and Robin worked full time at the bank until their first child, Megan, was born in 1982. The couple purchased a "starter" home when Megan was only 18 months old. Their second child, Matthew, followed a year later in 1986.

Like half of all American couples, Robin and Larry got divorced. The children were four-years-old and six-months-old, respectively. The divorce agreement was fairly standard; Robin got the house and custody of the children. She also was responsible for the house payment and all the home mainte-nance bills. Larry was awarded liberal visitation, ordered to pay $75 per week in child support, and got the newest car. He agreed to cover the children on his health insurance through his employer.

Then Robin went back to work full time at the bank. Larry visited the children and paid child support consistently for the first six months after the divorce. Then, the payments suddenly stopped—without explanation. (Note: The national average for regular payment of child support following divorce is six months; a study in Bexlar, Texas showed an 84% default rate at six months.)

When the child support payments stopped, Robin no longer had enough income to cover the mortgage or day care, food, clothing, and utility bills. Her parents helped out when they could, but within a year-and-a-half, the bank began foreclosure on the house, and Robin was devastated.

Robin, Matthew, and Megan are currently living in a small, rented apartment. They barely survive from month to month. Robin makes $200 a week at her $5-an-hour job. This is not enough to support the family and pay for day care, which is $100 per week for two pre-schoolers. Their family doctor will no longer see the children when they are ill because Larry removed them from his health care insurance (again, without explanation).

Robin went to the government Child Support Enforcement Agency when Larry stopped paying support in 1987. They told her they would bring Larry into court for a hearing, but this never happened. The County Sheriff only serves legal notices between 8 A.M. and 3 P.M., and never serves papers at work. In fact, the Sheriff told Robin that serving Larry his papers at work "would only embarrass him, and then he'd never pay support."

Robin believes she will have to quit her job and go on welfare if one of the children gets sick, or if the car needs repairs again, or if she continues to be behind on day care payments. Robin is worried and scared most of the time.

Megan and Matthew are only two of the more than 10 million children who have court orders for support but do not receive payments due to inefficiencies of the system.

CHILDREN FROM FAMILIES
WHOSE PARENTS WERE NEVER MARRIED

American Statistic: The number of children born to never-married parents in the U.S. has increased 377%.

Renee was 18 when she had her son, Jimmy. His father, Bill, was 20 and employed at a local automotive repair shop. Renee and Bill had been living together for about a year when Jimmy was born. Renee dropped out of computer school while she was expecting Jimmy because she felt it was the right thing to do. When Renee had Jimmy, Bill visited at the hospital and seemed to be proud and happy to have a son.

But when Renee brought the baby home from the hospital, it became apparent that Bill and Renee's lifestyle would drastically change. Bill said he "wasn't ready to settle down," that Renee was always tired and wasn't any fun. So, Bill moved out when Jimmy was six months old.

Renee applied for welfare when Bill left, because she had no money for rent or food. When she completed the Aid To Families With Dependent Children (AFDC) application at the welfare office, she was required to fill out an assignment of rights for child support to the state. She was told that in order to receive her AFDC check she must cooperate to establish paternity (fatherhood). She was entitled to receive a welfare check and the first $50 paid each month in child support by Bill, or the full amount of child support, whichever was more, after paternity was established.

Renee gave the welfare caseworker Bill's full name, address, and place of employment. Bill and Renee continued to see each other and dated regularly for a year. Occasionally, Bill would buy formula or diapers for Jimmy.

Renee knew she could not earn enough money on her own to support Jimmy. She saw very little hope of getting off welfare; being on it was difficult, and Renee felt isolated. She couldn't afford a telephone, and she was dependent on friends for a ride to the store. Her family rarely talked to her; they were angry that she had gotten pregnant and not finished school.

Renee learned how to survive on AFDC—she would buy her friends extra food so that they could buy her toothpaste, bar soap, and shampoo, since these items cannot be bought with food stamps. She also got extra help from the Welfare Department's Women, Infant, and Children Program so that she had formula, milk, and juice for Jimmy on a regular basis. She learned how to wait all day at the doctor's office for Jimmy to get a checkup, because few doctors accept patients on Medicaid.

Renee dreams about going back to school, getting a good job, and having the money to buy Jimmy the things he needs.

Two years after Jimmy was born, Renee and Bill stopped seeing each other. The Welfare Department, who had required Renee to provide information about Bill at the time of application, had taken no action during this time to establish paternity because cases were "backlogged."

When Jimmy was three, Renee received a letter from the government Child Support Agency. They asked her for updated information about Jimmy's father, but Renee had none to offer. She no longer knew where Bill lived or worked since he never came over to see Jimmy anymore.

Jimmy is one of more than 10 million children in the U.S. who need paternity established, who is living with a young mother dependent upon welfare to survive.

OVERVIEW

ACES, the Association For Children For Enforcement Of Support, was started in 1984 to help families like these. Our belief is that, by learning our legal rights and by organizing in our local communities, we can make sure our children receive much-needed child support payments.

Non-support affects over 16 million children in the U.S. who suffer a lack of adequate food, clothing, shelter, health care, and educational opportunities due to a parent's failure to pay child support. More children in this country live in poverty than ever before. One-half of all children born in 1991 will spend part of their lives growing up in single-parent households.

Nine out of every ten children on welfare are entitled to child support and do not receive those payments; $18 billion in accumulated unpaid child support is owed to these youngsters.

For those able to work, there is no acceptable excuse for failing to support their own children. Problems with custody, visitation, and other financial obligations are unacceptable excuses. Withholding support payments to strike back at an ex-spouse only steals food from a child's mouth. Non-support is a crime against children which must be stopped, and those who commit this crime should be punished accordingly.

Innovative enforcement methods, such as reporting a non-payor to the credit bureau to adversely affect his or her credit, "sweeps" to arrest the non-payor, and posting of the names of those who abandon their children (à la "Most Wanted" posters) all help, but much more has to be done.

ACES has found that when parents organize in their communities and demand that an effective and efficient child support enforcement program be implemented, the collection rate goes from 30% to 70%. ACES hopes that by parents getting involved and demanding action, we will end this crime against children and begin to eliminate child poverty.

The issue is not whether a parent should support his or her child, or should parents who break the law be prosecuted. Prosecution cannot further alienate parents who have already demonstrated that they don't care if their own children go to bed hungry. The issue is: Can and will government agencies effectively enforce child support laws and protect our children's futures?

ACES is a national organization which works every day to make sure all that can be done is being done to help children receive regular and adequate support payments.

PART I
THE BASICS OF CHILD SUPPORT

1. Money Makes the World Go 'Round

Who Can Collect Child Support and How Much Should Be Paid

Letter received from ACES in New Mexico (1990):

"I was watching the television and left the room for a few minutes. When I walked back in, ACES was being discussed on a popular daytime show. After listening to Geraldine Jensen talk about ACES, I thought I would write and see if you could help me. My story is that I was divorced in 1983 when my daughter was five-years-old. Her father has never given her anything to speak of other than a lot of empty promises. She is now almost 15-years-old.

I have always provided what I could for her, but it was not always easy. The time I contacted the Child Support Enforcement agency, I was told they could not locate my ex-husband and had no way to get the child support my daughter was owed. I did not, and still do not, have the money to try and track him down, nor the money to hire an attorney to do the same. It's not easy to take him to court when he keeps moving around the country and has done so for almost the last ten years.

I recently talked to a lady who managed, with your help, to collect back support for her two children long after she thought she would never get anything. Please let me know if this is possible, because I feel my daughter deserves a better chance at life. She and I both realize that without a college education, a better life is not realistic. Any information you could send me would help."

WERE YOU EVER ON WELFARE?
IS THERE CHILD SUPPORT OWED
TO THE STATE OR TO YOU?

IF YOU ANSWERED "yes" to the above questions, it is important that you understand your legal rights about what amount of child support is owed to you and what part is owed to the state. When you sign up for welfare (AFDC) you are required to assign your rights to child support over to the state. You may not have to do this if you do not want the welfare department to pursue the child support.

The only reasons the welfare department will allow you to refuse child support are if you can prove that you and your children would be in physical danger from the non-payor, or that you were a victim of incest or rape. In some states, if an adoption of the child is pending, they consider it good cause not to pursue child support.

Most people want the child support collected because they do not want to stay on welfare. Assignment of rights to child support means that you accept that the welfare check you receive is the state paying the child support for the non-payor, and that the state will pay itself back the amount they gave you in welfare from the non-payor. You do not owe the money to the state; the non-payor owes the money to the state.

States are only allowed to collect the amount of welfare money given to you or the amount of child support that should have been paid when you were on welfare, whichever is less.

For example, if you received $300 a month in welfare and your child support order was $400 a month, the state is only entitled to $300. If your welfare check was $300 a month and the child support order was $250 a month, the state is only entitled to $250 a month.

If the non-custodial parent pays support while you are on welfare, you are entitled to the first $50 paid each month in addition to your welfare check.

Many ACES members report that no payment were made while they were on welfare, or only partial payments were made. When these families go off welfare and child support is collected, often there are problems concerning who gets the child support—the family or the state. Federal law allows states to pay families their back support first. However, most states do not do this, they use many different types of complicated formulas to determine who gets the back support.

Most states follow this procedure: The families get all *current* support and payments on back support that accumulated *before* they got on welfare and *after* they got off welfare. The state then gets payments on back support that accumulated while the family was on welfare.

Some states, such as Ohio, pay all the families' back support before collecting back support owed to the state. Pennsylvania pays all back support collected to the state first.

It is important that you check the records at your welfare department and child support agency to make sure they are following the correct procedure to calculate your back support and the support owed to the state. You can request an audit of your case to see how this was calculated.

If you feel that the state is claiming back support to which you are not entitled, you can request a "state fair hearing" or "state administrative hearing" at the welfare department.

This will ensure that the state meets with you and, in detail, explains how they calculated the back support. They will give you the opportunity to express your concerns. You can take a friend to the fair hearing to help you. Or, contact Legal Aid; they will help you if you qualify for their services.

Any support collected by attaching non-payor's federal income tax is used to pay off any back support owed to the welfare department before it is used to pay off back support owed to the family. This is an exception to all other rules states have, and it is a good way to get that old welfare arrearage paid off.

Monies collected may be of an amount large enough so that the family gets some of it for back support owed to them. If you feel confused about this issue, don't feel bad. The only stupid question is the one not asked!

Getting Support

More children than ever before are living in poverty in the U.S. The major contributing factor is failure of parents to meet child support obligations.

Many families are forced onto the "welfare rolls," and 87% of families receiving Aid to Families With Dependent Children are not receiving regular child support payments.

As a result, children who have been abandoned by one parent suffer economically as well as emotionally. Single parents, too, face increased stress and anxiety over seemingly overwhelming responsibilities and financial hardships.

It often seems the problems are insurmountable, but they aren't—changing legislation and organizations like ACES are proof that help is available.

ACES provides educational information concerning child support and visitation. This information includes your legal rights and remedies, which agency to contact for assistance, both local and interstate (out-of-state), methods available under current law to collect current and back child support, and methods available under current law to resolve visitation problems.

Don't give up on your case! There are many alternatives and options available. Know your rights and be persistent and firm when dealing with public agencies and attorneys. They are working for you and must represent your case to the best of their ability. You can help by providing as much evidence, witnesses, etc., to make your case as strong as possible. And make sure the person representing you presents your evidence in court.

For further information you may contact the ACES Chapter Coordinator nearest you and/or the chapter nearest where the non-payor lives (if the non-payor is out-of-state, the chapter in the other state can give you information about that state's child support enforcement laws and procedures) See the chapter list in the Appendix or contact ACES National Office in Toledo, Ohio at (800)537-7072.

HOW MUCH SHOULD BE PAID

By October of 1989 all states were required under federal law to use a mathematical formula to determine how much child support should be paid.

This ended years of judges and attorneys being able to decide how much should be paid based on "deals" being made as part of a divorce, or arbitrary decisions by judges which often resulted in orders that read: $25 a week for one child, $50 a week for two children, and $75 a week for three children. These often unfair and unreasonable child support orders can now be updated under the Child Support guidelines.

Child Support guidelines are a rebuttable presumption— this mean that they (the guidelines) must be followed and be part of the court order for child support unless a judge or administrative hearing officer states in writing why they should not be followed. The deviation from the guidelines can be upward or downward, based on the situation. For example, one reason a child support order could be less than the Child Support guidelines would be when a non-custodial parent is making the house payment on the house in which the child lives, in addition to regular child support payments. The child support amount could be more than the guidelines amount if a child has special medical needs and not all costs of his or her medical care were covered under health insurance.

There are two basic types of mathematical formulas used for child support guidelines in the U.S.: percentage guidelines and combined income guidelines.

A percentage guideline means that the non-custodial parent pays a specific percentage of his or her income for child support. For example, in Wisconsin, the percentage guidelines are based on gross income. A parent pays 17% for one child, 25% for two children, 29% for three children, 31% for four children, and 34% for more than four children. In Delaware, the parents pay a percentage of net income: 18% for one child, 27% for two children, 35% for three children, 40% for four children, 45% for five children, and 50% for six or more children.

Combined income guidelines are when both the custodial and non-custodial parents' income are used to determine how much support is paid. This guideline adds both parental incomes together. The combined amount is then compared to a chart listing the cost of raising children on that combined income. The amount it costs to raise the children is then divided proportionately between the parents. For example:

Mom's annual earnings: $10,000
Dad's annual earnings: $30,000
Combined earnings: $40,000

The combined income guidelines chart would show that, if this family had two children, the cost of raising the children in a family with a $40,000 per year income would be $9,000. This amount is then divided between the parents based on the percentage each has of the combined amount. Since mom earned $10,000 of the $40,000, she is responsible for $\frac{1}{4}$ or 25% of the $9,000 cost of raising the children. Since Dad earned $30,000 of the $40,000, he is responsible for $\frac{3}{4}$ or 75% of the $9,000 cost of raising the children.

This means that Mom would be responsible for $2,250 and Dad would be responsible for $6,750.

If the mother is the custodial parent:

Income $10,000
Child Support   6,750
            $16,750

If the father is the custodial parent:

Income $30,000
Child Support   2,250
            $32,250

In addition to the basic child support amount, a judge or administrative hearing officer can order a parent to provide additional support for cost of day care, medical insurance, or health care of the child and other special needs.

You can obtain a copy of the child support guidelines used in your state by contacting your local Clerk Of Courts or your state Child Support Enforcement Agency.

By estimating the amounts of the parents' incomes on the child support guidelines worksheets for your state, you will be able to determine an approximate amount of support that a court or administrative hearing officer would order to be paid on your case. ACES research has shown that the average amount of child support paid ($40 per week) increased to at least $60 per week when the new support guidelines were applied.

You may be entitled to an increase in your support under the new Child Support guidelines. In some states, you must show that there has been a change in circumstance in addition to the fact that there are now child support guidelines.

Change of circumstance is defined differently in many states, but usually means that the child's needs have changed (i.e., food and clothing cost more because the child is older; the child is involved in special activities; or the child has special medical needs).

A child support increase or decrease can be granted by the court or administrative hearing officer due to change in parental income. If a non-custodial parent has lost his or her job and it is a long-term loss of employment, the court will usually order a lesser amount to support to be paid. If the custodial parent has lost his or her job, and it is a long-term loss of employment, the court will usually order the non-custodial parent to pay more child support.

In most states, if one of the parents is unemployed when a child support order is being established for the first time, the amount of income usually earned is used to determine the amount of support to be paid, or a minimum amount such as $50 per month will be demanded.

If you can prove to a judge that the non-custodial parent has voluntarily become unemployed, or has quit his or her job to avoid paying child support, the judge can base an order on what could be earned instead of what is earned.

Providing judges or administrative hearing officers with information about the true earnings of parents is essential for the child support guidelines to work in order to produce fair amounts of support.

The parent's earnings information should be provided to the court in the form of at least three paycheck stubs and a copy of last year's IRS return. If needed, the earnings information should be subpoenaed from the parent's employer. Also, if the parent is self-employed, the company books, bank accounts, and other business records can be subpoenaed to show a true income.

Most states allow assets such as IRAs, stocks, bonds, etc. to be counted when determining the parent's income. State child support guidelines define income in your state and gross or net income.

COLLECTING ALIMONY

All states, except Texas, have laws allowing spousal mainte-nance (alimony) orders. There have been many changes in alimony laws in the past ten years since no-fault divorce laws have been adopted by many states. It is more difficult than ever to obtain an alimony award in the 1990s due to changes in laws and in society generally.

Alimony or spousal support, as it is often called, is primarily designed to provide an ex-spouse with income for daily living expenses such as housing, food, clothing, etc.

Alimony can be long term or short term. Sometimes, the court orders alimony to be paid for three or four years while a parent attends school so that he or she can obtain to job to become more self-sufficient. Other times, alimony is ordered to be paid for a lifetime.

In most states, alimony court orders can be enforced in the same way as child support, through income withholding, posting of bonds to ensure payments, and through execution of judgments against personal or real property. Sale and seizure of the car of a non-payor, placement of a lien on real estate, and forcing foreclosure are some other available methods of ensuring alimony when it is necessary.

You can represent yourself in court to enforce an alimony order, hire a private attorney, or you may be eligible for enforcement action through a IV-D agency if they are also enforcing a child support order for you.

Usually, a court will order alimony if you were a homemaker during the marriage and you have no outside income or skills necessary to support yourself. Alimony can also be ordered if there are young children and the custodial parent cannot earn enough money to support the family and pay day care.

Maintenance or spousal support is counted as income for tax purposes. It is tax-deductible for the one who pays alimony if it is paid in cash under the terms of a written agreement. The couple may not live together and may not file a joint income tax return.

2. God Bless Uncle Sam
Getting the Government Child Support Enforcement Agency To Help You

"I think if you're just starting to try to collect support, you should go to the IV-D Agency first. I don't advocate getting a private attorney—they're expensive, ineffective, and most of the time you wind up spending ten years in order to enforce two or three months of your child support. Also, private attorneys don't have access to parent locator services, and they can't do interstate income withholding. But you still have to make sure that you constantly follow up on the agency.

"I've had to go in as an ACES Chapter Coordinator and show the agencies how to clean up the messes that the agencies have caused!"

—B.B., Sandy, Oregon

TITLE IV-D (4-D) of the Federal Social Security Act of 1975 established a local IV-D child support agency in every U.S. state and jurisdiction. This agency is located at various government departments. (See Appendix B for state IV-D child support enforcement offices). Services are provided to all, whether or not you receive Aid To Families With Dependent Children.

Under the federal child support laws, the maximum fee that can be charged for services through Title IV-D is $25.

Services provided are as follows:

1. Location of the absent parent and/or assets through the Federal Parent Locator Service.

The IV-D agency has access to the following types of records: IRS, social security, motor vehicle departments, Veterans Administration, Department of Defense, credit bureaus, real estate, voter registration, criminal records, postal records, and loan companies.

2. Enforcement of a court order through wage withholding, contempt proceedings, liens, judgments, posting of cash bonds, and modifications.

3. Establishment of a court order for paternity (fatherhood).

4. Establishment of an order if you are separated.

5. Establishment and enforcement of medical support.

6. Enforcement of alimony if in the same order as the child support.

7. Attachment of federal and state income tax refunds.

   a. Arrearage must be $150 if you are an AFDC recipient or $500 if not an AFDC recipient.

   b. Payor is advised of the attachment and can appeal based on mistake-of-fact only.

8. Attachment of unemployment compensation.

9. Attachment of military wages, retirement benefits, or V.A. benefits.

10. Modification (change) of a court order for an increase or decrease on the amount of support paid.

PART II

CHOOSING HELP

3. What Do You Mean I have to Go To Court?

"I never thought I had to go to court to get support for my children. I just took it for granted that, since it said in our divorce decree that he had to pay $500 a month, he would do it. Now that I know my rights and a little bit more about how the system works, I'm going to court to get my children the money they're entitled to."

—H.M., Buffalo, New York

TO COLLECT CHILD support, you must first have a court order from a divorce, dissolution, establishment of paternity, or legal separation.

All states have a Child Support Enforcement Agency that is federally funded and must help you to collect support if your children are under 18 or if you apply for help before the child turns 18, for a maximum $25 fee.

This agency must provide you with a "free" attorney if needed. Contact your welfare department and ask for the name and address of the Child Support Agency (IV-D Agency).

If you do not have a court order for child support, you can contact your local Child Support Enforcement Agency (IV-D) and request that they establish an order. This can be done by establishing paternity if you were not married.

The Agency can establish an order for you if you are

separated or have been deserted. You do not have to be divorced for the IV-D agency to help you get a court order. You can also do this through a private attorney or by representing yourself.

4. Working with Attorneys to Collect Support

"It was expensive to hire an attorney, and even after it was over, I didn't really get anything. When I turned to ACES for help, I found out I had all kinds of rights that the attorneys never told me about.

The IV-D agencies don't give you any idea what they can do for you . . . it's almost like you have to educate yourself to be your own attorney.

There are all kinds of things you should know about hiring an attorney, if that's what you really want to do. Make sure you educate yourself so you know what to look for. That way, you won't have to go through what I did. I actually had to hire another attorney to get the first one off my back!"

— D.F., Chicago, Illinois

AT ONE TIME or another, almost every child support case needs some sort of action that requires a court hearing. When this occurs, you must make the decision whether you will use the services of an attorney from the local Child Support Agency, hire a private attorney to handle your case, or represent yourself in court.

All local government IV-D Child Support Agencies in each state have attorneys that provide legal representation for child support issues. These agency attorneys may be local county attorneys (prosecutors, district attorneys) or state attorneys (assistant attorney generals) who are under cooperative agreements with the state or county to provide services. Or, they may be private attorneys under contract with the agency to provide services, or attorneys who have actually been hired by the Agency and are part of its staff.

There are no income eligibility requirements, and a maximum fee of $25 may be charged to use the services of the Agency's attorney. All that is required is that you sign a IV-D application.

Services that IV-D attorneys provide:

1.—Establishing paternity.

2.—Establishing new court orders or modifying current ones.

3.—Handling both in-state and out-of-state cases.

4.—Enforcing child support orders that have become delinquent through use of income withholding, liens, judgments (and to execute judgments by filing levies against property, houses, boats, cars, etc.), cash bonds, or lump sum payments.

5.—Establishing medical support orders by requiring non-custodial parents to place the children on health insurance coverage provided by an employer and enforcing the medical support orders.

The IV-D attorney can bring civil contempt charges (often called a "motion to show cause") against a non-payor and file criminal non-support charges if she is a county attorney. The agency attorneys are not responsible for and will not provide services for custody and/or visitation issues. You will need to obtain a private attorney for these cases.

The IV-D attorneys are responsible for gathering all needed legal evidence to present the case in court through use of subpoenas, depositions, and interrogatories.

The attorneys are also responsible for making sure that all necessary legal notices are sent out to all parties involved in the hearing, and providing representation at all pre-trial hearings.

Once a case goes to hearing before a judge or court master, referee or commissioner (these are attorneys hired by the court to handle hearings so that cases can be processed faster) and a decision is filed that you believe is an incorrect interpretation of the law, the child support attorney is responsible for filing objections to the decisions. (This usually needs to be within 10–14 days after the decision is filed. Check with your local courts to find out exactly how long the period is to file these objections.)

This means that your case can now be heard in front of a judge. IV-D attorneys are also responsible for filing appeals to judges' orders which are being disputed. This usually must be done within 30 days after the order becomes final.

If there is to be a court hearing held out-of-state, IV-D attorneys provide the same services as if you actually resided where the case is being heard.

For example: parent and child live in California, and non-payor lives in Missouri. California sends the legal paperwork to Missouri. Your case is taken into court by the IV-D attorney in Missouri.

If you have a case going to court in another state, make sure that you find out who the attorney is that is handling the case. Write the attorney a letter explaining what you want accomplished at the hearing and send a picture of your children, too. Let the attorney know that there are actually faces behind the names that they are representing.

Recently, there has been some debate across the nation on who the IV-D attorney is actually representing. Are they representing you as a client, your children, or the state? Most of the government child support agencies take the position that they are neither representing you nor your children, that they are actually representing the state.

How does this affect you? Simply put, what they are trying to do is say that an "attorney-client" relationship does not exist between you and the IV-D attorney. ACES disputes this opinion. Our attorneys believe there is an attorney-client relationship even if state laws say the IV-D attorney represents the state: This is an ethical issue, not a legal one. ACES believes that if the IV-D attorney provides the same services as a private attorney then they are "your attorney."

Your Options

Pro se (*self representation in court*) According to the law, you may file your own motions and represent yourself in court. You can request a contempt of court hearing, wage withholding, judgment, etc. by completing proper court petitions. (See Appendix for samples.)

Pro bono (*free attorney assigned to you by the Bar Association if you cannot afford an attorney and are low income*) or Legal Aide attorney (available in some states) These attorneys file motions and will represent you in a court hearing for contempt, wage withholding, judgment, etc.

Private attorney (*paid hourly or receives a percentage of what is collected*) The attorney files motions and will represent you in all of the same procedures as listed above. You can make arrangements to pay the attorney a percentage of what is collected, such as 20–30% if there is a large arrearage.

MAKE A "SHOPPING LIST"

If you decide that you would rather hire a private attorney because you want special attention or need one for visitation and/or custody matters, you should begin shopping around for an attorney.

Make a "shopping list" of your needs. You want someone who knows what they are doing—do not pay for someone to be their "test" case.

1. Ask around and prepare a list of those attorneys that may qualify. Find other people who have used a private attorney

for the same reason you need one. Talk with them to find out what happened in their particular cases. Was the attorney easy to reach? Did they return telephone calls? How does the attorney treat their clients? Do they actually take time to listen and do what is asked of them or do they take action without first consulting the client? Did they take the time to explain things in ways that could be understood? Did they really seem to care?

2. Prepare questions to ask the attorney.

a. Do they know how to obtain a lien, judgment, bond, etc.?

b. Do they know what the current laws say on custody or visitation issues?

c. How much do they charge for services?

d. Is there a fee for initial consultation?

e. Is there a retainer (money to be paid upfront)?

f. Will they take a case on a contingency basis (they only get a percentage of any money that is collected)?

g. Can you set up a payment plan?

It is usually a better idea to hire an attorney that lives in the same town or county where the case is being heard. This is especially true if you live in a smaller city or town, because there can be a prejudice against a "hot-shot" attorney from a large city out of your area. Local attorneys and judges all know one another and it is always better to have a "home court advantage."

You should always try to find out if there is any sort of relationship between the attorney that you hire and that of the opposing side. Ask the attorney that you are thinking of hiring if he/she has ever represented the non-custodial parent in any type of legal matter, or if he/she has any friendly or unfriendly dealings with the non-custodial parent's attorney. Ask if your attorney has any scores to settle or any grudges against the opposing counsel or vice versa.

Remember, a private attorney is working for you. You

hired them. Tell her/him what you expect to gain from the court proceedings.

If it is suggested that you accept an offer from the opposing side, make sure it is something you can really live with—you cannot appeal the decision to the court. Do not accept any offer until you're positive it's fair!

PART III

METHODS OF COLLECTION

5. Locating the Non-Payor

"We started trying to locate my ex-husband back in February of 1991 and we haven't been able to find him yet . . . but if he's got a busted taillight or something, he hasn't got a prayer!

We went to court every year prior to his disappearance. After our fourth time in court, the judge ordered five days in jail for every missed payment. He fled instead of paying the support.

The most frustrating part is: What is this doing to my daughter, who's only nine-years-old? I've since remarried, and we have money coming in and a decent home life. But I'm concerned for her emotional well-being.

Like many women in the South, I was raised to be subservient and to never question my husband. I'm not real big on confrontations. I don't want him to have to go to jail or anything. I just want him to know that you can't just do this kind of thing and get away with it."
—G.J., Huntsville, Alabama

OKAY, SO YOU know that your children deserve the child support, but in order to get the money you must find the absent parent. This chapter includes information about finding the absent parent's whereabouts and location of income and assets.

To obtain a court order or to enforce a court order for child support, legal documents must be delivered to the absent parent notifying them of the legal action which will take place. This legal "service of notice" is a constitutional right. It is designed to protect citizens from wrongful accusations and fraud.

This protects your legal rights, too. The absent parent cannot change child support to a lower amount payable unless you have been legally notified of the proposed action and have been given the opportunity to present your side of the story.

Location of the absent parent's place of employment, income and assets is necessary to have in order to obtain payments. If the employer is known, a pay check can be attached. This income withholding or payroll deduction to collect child support is very effective. If bank accounts are located, they can be attached to collect current or back support payments. An effective and thorough investigation to determine the absent parent's whereabouts and assets are essential to obtaining child support payments.

DOING YOUR HOMEWORK

"I thought we would never locate my children's father, never collect any of the $9,000 in back support due. But with ACES' help, group action, and persistence, I was proved wrong! Last month, all $9,000 was paid."

—S.C., Atlanta, Georgia

You can do much of the investigation on your own, even though state child support agencies are required to do investigation to help you locate an absent parent.

Keep a list of information about the absent parent handy and update it periodically. You may need to locate the absent parent more than once before you successfully collect child support. Persistence pays—sometimes, quite handsomely.

Some types of resources to help you locate the absent parent are available at your local library. These include telephone directories from cities in your area as well as those of cities throughout the U.S. City directories list occupation, place of employment, addresses, and phone numbers.

"Backwards" directories, or "R. L. Polk" directories, also include listings by phone numbers that show the address where the phone is located. Government offices and private agencies including the Recorder's Office, Voter Registration, Department Of Motor Vehicles, Post Office, Secretary Of State, occupational/professional organizations, trade unions, high schools, trade schools or colleges, and military locator services, offer further options.

Recorder's Office: Lists deeds (ownership) to property.

Treasurer's Office And/Or Property Tax Office: Lists values of property.

Fishing And Hunting Licenses/Bureaus: Used as a source in some states that centralize these records in a county or state office.

Voter Registration: These records are open to the public and list home addresses.

Department Of Motor Vehicles: In most states, for approximately $3.00, the Department will provide you with an address and a list of vehicles registered in the name of the absent parent.

Send them a written request for the information and be sure to include the absent parent's full name, last known address, date of birth, and social security number (if known). You can do this even if you live in one state and the absent parent's last known address is in another state. Send the request to the state of the non-payor's last known address.

Post Office: For a $1.00 fee, the U.S. Postal Service will do a postal verification. This service takes about two weeks. The Post Office will inform you if the absent parent regularly receives mail at any address you ask them to check. The absent parent is not informed by the Post Office that their address is being verified.

Also available through the Post Office is information about

change of address. Send a letter with a notation on the envelope that states "address correction requested."

The Post Office will charge you 25 cents if they forward the letter to the absent parent and send you a notice of the address change. Since you have to send a letter to the absent parent with a return address on it to use this method, the absent parent will know you are looking for him or her.

Secretary Of State: Keeps records of corporations within the state and home-based foreign corporations that are located in a different state but registered within the state in question. These records include addresses of the corporations and a listing of corporate officers or registered agent(s).

Occupational And Professional License Bureaus have listings of addresses and places of employment. These could include doctors, nurses, pharmacists, insurance agents, stock brokers, etc. Also, some state organizations for professionals may be able to verify a place of employment or provide you with information to contact an absent parent.

Trade Unions can provide a list of companies currently employing union members. This can assist you in verifying the place of employment of an absent person. Union records which show when union dues were payroll-deducted can be subpoenaed and used in court to show a work record and the ability to pay support.

Absent Parent's High School, Trade school, or College Alumni Office may have a current address on file. They may also be a source of the birth-date and social security number of the absent parent.

State and Federal Parent Locator Services

You can complete an application at your state or local Child Support Enforcement Agency. The maximum application fee for child support enforcement is $25.00, and this is for full services. Locate-only services are available for $5.00.

All states are required to check state records to attempt to locate an absent parent within 75 days of your request. Records checked can include the Department of Motor Vehicles, state welfare records, Department of Corrections, State Employment/Labor Department, state tax records, State Worker's Compensation Departments, Health Departments and, criminal records kept by local law enforcement agencies are also available.

A state parent locator should be done in the state of the last known address of the absent parent. Government studies show that 52% of all absent parents are located in the same state as the last known address, or at least an adjacent state.

Some states have cooperation agreements with surrounding states via shared computer databases. Florida, Alabama, Georgia, Mississippi, North Carolina, South Carolina, Virginia, and Ohio can check each other's state records via a computer terminal in the state child support agencies. Oregon, Washington, Montana, Idaho, and Alaska also share a database of locator information.

For example, if you live in New York and the last known address of the absent parent is in California, you need to request that the New York Child Support Enforcement Agency do a state parent locator in California.

Under federal law, within 20 days of your request, New York would have to send a written request to California to do the state parent locator. California must do the state parent locator within 75 days of the request.

Federal parent locators access IRS records, social security records, U.S. Department of Labor records, Veterans Administration, Department of Defense, and federal employee records. A state child support agency must access the federal parent locator service if parent locator sources fail to find an absent parent. They can do a federal parent locator and a state parent locator simultaneously.

If state and federal parent locators fail to find the absent parent, the government agencies are required to automatically investigate the sources every quarter for three years. If, after three years of quarterly attempts the parent locators remain unsuccessful, they can close the child support case. However, the case must be reopened if any new information is made available (if you locate the non-payor).

Obtaining Information From Friends, Relatives, And Neighbors

You can determine the phone number of a non-payor's neighbor, if you know their address, by looking up the addresses near the non-payor in a Criss-Cross Directory (also known as a city directory, backwards directory, etc.) found at the local library.

For example, if the non-payor lives at 1234 Oak St., you can look up 1236 Oak St. in the directory and call the non-payor's neighbor. You can then ask the neighbor if they know where the non-payor works.

You or someone acting on your behalf can ask the non-payor's relatives where the non-payor's place of employment is located. Often people will give this information when asked if they have the daytime phone number of the non-payor.

Innovative Investigation Techniques

When all else fails, get sneaky! Check the contents of the non-payor's trash. The U.S. Supreme Court has ruled that once trash is "put out to the curb," it becomes public property. Therefore, it is not illegal to take the trash and check it out for information about the non-payor, such as the names of banks and creditors.

You can also subpoena a loan application to obtain a listing of assets of the non-payor.

I had a friend pretend she was conducting a phone survey. She asked my ex-husband some questions, which he ended up answering. We found out all we wanted to know!

—G.J., Toledo, O.H.

Let your fingers do the walking. To call someone on the phone and ask them survey questions is not illegal unless you mislead the person by saying you are from a business. If you say, "Hello, I'm doing a survey about your favorite cars, would you mind taking a few minutes to answer some questions?" and the person volunteers to answer, it is perfectly legal.

You can ask about income: $10,000–$15,000; $15,000–$25,000; $25,000–$30,000, etc. Ask about age, type of employment, where employed, etc. to solicit information about income and assets of the non-payor. ACES members have done this with a high degree of success.

Establishing Paternity

"Thanks, ACES, for your information and guidance, which led to the establishment of paternity for my son. I had thought the case was hopeless because the father lived in Canada. But ACES showed me how to collect support even though it was international!"

—S.T., Ohio

What is paternity establishment? It is a process that formally and legally links a child with his or her father.

Establishment of paternity means that the mother was not married to the father when the child was born and a legal agreement (court order) is obtained which states a certain man is the father of a certain child.

Establishing paternity can also take place if the couple was married but living apart when the child was conceived.

Why should I establish paternity, you might wonder? Children benefit from paternity in many ways:

1. Child support payments will be a right so that the child grows up having the things he or she needs.

2. The father's health insurance covers the child.

3. The father's estate passes to the child through Social Security benefits.

4. The child is legitimate.

5. The child has full heritage and knows he or she has a complete family.

Why should you establish paternity when you and the father are still seeing each other and he helps out by buying diapers and food? The answer is because no one knows what the future will be. Your child needs you to take action to protect his or her future.

Studies show that fathers of children born to mothers who are teenagers frequently have little or no income when the baby is born. However, these same fathers had incomes of $15,000 a year or more within the next five years. Mothers who took no action when the child was born had difficulty establishing paternity later on because they had lost contact with the father.

If you think that because you're collecting welfare you aren't eligible to also receive child support payments, you're wrong. Sometimes, the child support will be more than the welfare check and you will still be able to receive food stamps, day care assistance, and other benefits in addition to the child support.

Hopefully, you will be able to get a good job and not need the welfare in the future. Many mothers need their pay check and the child support to pay bills and provide day care for the child so they can work.

"The child support payments meant that Tonya could have a nice dress for Christmas from the Lion Store rather than hand-me-downs.

I could buy pictures of her to treasure the memory of her youth. When Tonya was six-months-old, it was diapers and baby food she needed. When she was three, I was worried about money for a good pre-school. Now that she's a teenager, it's designer clothes so that she can feel good about herself. Next it will be money for college so she can have a better life and not spend her life worrying about how to make ends meet like I have."

—I.D., Albuquerque, New Mexico

HOW TO ESTABLISH PATERNITY

1. Fill out an application at the Department of Human Services if you receive welfare benefits or at the Child Support Enforcement Agency if you do not receive welfare.

2. No matter where you completed the application, call the Child Support Enforcement Agency and ask to speak to your enforcement officer about the case.

Ask the officer the following questions:

★What have you done on my paternity case so far?

★Have you contacted the father to ask him to voluntarily sign the paternity papers? If yes, ask when this will happen. If no, ask the officer to contact him. If the answer is yes, but the alleged father refuses to sign, ask your officer to schedule blood tests (HLA) for you, the child, and the alleged father. If the blood tests are positive, the court will issue a paternity court order even if the father continues to object.

The paternity court order should include a statement that the alleged is indeed the child's father; a child support order, such as $25 per week; and a statement that the father is to put the child on his health insurance (if possible).

Paternity court orders do not include visitation unless the father asks for it to be included. It is not automatic and you can ask the court referee to order supervised visitation if you think the father will not be able to take care of the child alone or if you think the child would not be safe with the father.

Court actions to establish paternity usually take place in

Juvenile Court. If the man agrees he is the father of a child born out of wedlock, a court action may not be necessary.

An attorney can draw up a legal document which both parents sign. In the document, it should state that the man is the child's father, the amount he agrees to pay for child support, whether he agrees to pay medical bills incurred from the child's birth, whether he agrees to provide medical insurance for the child, and possibly a visitation agreement.

These agreements vary widely between couples and must be approved by the court. A judge will sign the agreement, and it will be filed with the Clerk of Courts—then it is considered official. If you are entering into a paternity agreement, be sure to assess the needs of the child carefully in order to best protect your child's future.

A man can request a jury trial if he denies paternity. If this occurs, the IV-D attorney can represent you, or you can be represented by a private attorney. Evidence will be introduced by your attorney and his attorney. The jury will review the evidence and make a decision regarding paternity. Jury trials are sometimes long and are more difficult for the mother to endure.

Sometimes an attorney or the father will use a threat of jury trial just to intimidate the mother. If you are going to have to participate in a jury trial, seek support of friends, relatives, and/or advocacy groups such as ACES to assist you and provide you with moral support.

After you have established paternity and the father has been ordered to make support payments, all remedies under current law are available to you to enforce your child support order.

6. Right Off the Top
Payroll Deductions

"I signed up for IV-D services when I went off of AFDC after going back to school and then back to work. I worked for six months, and then the child support stopped.

I pressured the IV-D agency constantly (which I strongly suggest doing) until, finally, they did go after the wage withholding. It took me about three months—which was a lot longer than it should have taken.

But, now that I do have wage withholding, I don't have to go back on AFDC. I have two separate court orders for two separate fathers, since I have two children by one father and one by another. But they're both wage withholdings, and it's been working wonderfully."

—R.G., St. Paul, Minnesota

Methods To Enforce a Court Order: Income Withholding

IF THE NON-PAYOR is employed and you know where he/she is working, federal law P.L. 98–378 requires mandatory wage withholding for child support payments of arrearages equal to one month or more.* Example: If the

---

*New federal laws will allow for income withholding at the time of divorce or establishment of paternity by November 1, 1990 for IV-D cases; all other cases by January 1, 1994.

court order is $300 per month, when the payor becomes $300 delinquent, a wage withholding should be done.

Procedure To Obtain a Wage Withholding:

1. Apply at your local IV-D agency. If you are not a IV-D case and choose not to apply to IV-D, your state may have a law that says you can seek a wage withholding order by yourself or through a private attorney.

2. Request a wage withholding for enforcement from employer.

3. The IV-D agency should file the appropriate legal documents for you to obtain a wage withholding order.

4. The employer and non-payor will be advised of the wage withholding amount and frequency.

5. Employers are liable for the amount of support to be withheld and must send payments to the child support agency at each pay period. They must also notify the child support agency of any change in employment status, and may not terminate or punish an employee because of a wage withholding order. The employer may withhold only the amounts allowed by the Consumer Credit Protection Act: 60% of wages plus 5% for arrearages of over 12 weeks if the non-payor is not remarried and has no dependents; and 50% of wages plus 5% for arrearages of over 12 weeks if the non-payor is remarried and has dependents.

The absent parents employer must forward payments to IV-D agency within 10 days.

Employers can be taken to court if they are non-compliant with a wage withholding order. The payor will be advised that the child support will be payroll deducted and the date it will begin.

The payor is also notified that the only way to stop the wage withholding is to request a mistake-of-fact hearing (this means wrong person—I don't owe support).

If no mistake-of-fact hearing is requested, the withholding begins. If the payor requests a hearing, you will be notified. If possible, you should attend to protect your interests.

"Persistence pays! My children finally collected almost $6,000 in back support. ACES helped me to get the child support system to work! Current support payments are being payroll deducted and back support was paid when the non-payor was threatened with a jail sentence."

—B.B., Tulsa, Oklahoma

INTERSTATE INCOME WITHHOLDING

"Finally, the wage withholding papers were sent to Florida and his wages were attached for child support. ACES made this happen. Before I became a member, I had been trying for three years to get action on my case. The Illinois child support system just kept telling me nothing could be done because he was out of state. ACES told me how to get Illinois and Florida to take action. The first child support check in almost five years is being processed right now!"

—S.S., Chicago, Illinois

Federal law requires all states to have laws for interstate wage withholding. The procedure usually includes sending three certified copies of the original court order, three copies of the wage withholding petition, and an affidavit of arrearages to the state IV-D agency where the non-payor lives.

Some states require more information. Check with the state child support agency where the non-payor resides.

This method is the best available to collect on interstate cases, but you must know the non-payor's place of employment and the non-payor must receive a regular pay check from a company for this procedure to be effective.

Your Child Support Enforcement Agency is required by federal law to investigate on your behalf to determine the non-payor's place of employment. Interstate income withholding is the quickest method on these types of cases and prohibits the state where the non-payor lives from changing (reducing) your court order, and helps ensure regular receipt of payments. This method should include payments on current support and payments on back support.*

*Note: New regulations require the state where you live to follow up on your case at least every 90 days. They also require the state where the non-payor lives to respond within 10 days of receipt of the paperwork to assist in locating absent parents via a state parent locator, within 75 days, and to process cases expeditiously. Your state must respond to requests for more information within 30 days. Both states must forward payments within 15 days of receipt of the child support.

PART IV

DEALING WITH DIFFICULT PROBLEMS

7. Just Across The Border
Collecting Across State Lines

"I trusted the system and it basically screwed me over. I got a judgment that says my ex-husband is supposed to be paying me $500 a month in child support, but he still chooses to pay only what he wants, which is $200 a month. I also got a judgment for $56,500 in back support, but this turned out to be wrong because the state of Maryland (where I live) and Washington, D.C. (where he lives) messed up by not adding up every month since we split up. They were only going by the figures I had previously given them which were by then three years old!

Ever since, I've been trying to get the right amount, which is now $67,800. But it's been such a long, frustrating situation! Not too long ago, they gave him a credit for $295, which wiped out all the back support and basically said he'd overpaid by $295. That's when I went in and asked them to audit my account. They sent those figures to D.C., who told me that my ex was not in arrears. I said, "Have you ever received that kind of money ($50,000 or more) from anybody?" Then, I was apologized to and told that there was some kind of computer error.

But I would have been adversely affected permanently if I had not asked for a copy of those records. My advice is: STAY ON THE AGENCIES' BACKS. Too often, these agencies are run by people who just want to collect a pay check. You always have to look out for yourself."

—B.C., Silver Springs, Maryland

THERE ARE THREE types of main actions which can be taken regarding interstate enforcement actions.

For other types of actions, contact the ACES National Office. There is always hope and there are many different options available to seek the support your children deserve.

Newest Methods

Interstate wage withholding. Use for collections of current support and payments on back support. This action can be started in some states by you and in all states by the local IV-D child support agency. You should know the non-payor's place of employment.

The usual procedure is to send the following to the local IV-D agency in the county where the non-payor lives:

a. Three certified copies of the original court order and any changes.
b. Three certified copies of the withholding order or petition to withhold.
c. A sworn affidavit from you which states arrearages.
d. A copy, if possible of a payment record from your Clerk of Courts or child support agency which collects and distributes payments.
e. The name and address of the non-payor.
f. The name and address of the non-payor's employer.
g. The name and address of the agency to whom payments should be sent.
h. A copy of your application for IV-D services if possible.

You should check with the ACES National Office or the State IV-D Agency where the non-payor lives for complete procedures.

URESA Method

The URESA (Uniform Reciprocal Enforcement Support Act) or Reciprocal is used for collection of back support, current support, medical expenses, and to obtain increases in the amount of support paid.

1. Apply to the IV-D program at your local child support agency or county attorney.

2. The IV-D attorney or county attorney will process the legal paperwork.

3. URESA paperwork is sent to the state/county where non-payor lives.

4. A court hearing is scheduled.

5. Non-payor is served with notice of the court hearing.

6. A hearing is held were non-payor lives; you do not have to be present.

7. The court reaches a decision and issues an order.

You should contact the county attorney in writing in the county where the non-payor lives and by phone if possible before the court date to make sure that service was obtained and to tell the person representing you your side of the story. A nice letter with pictures of the children should help add a more personal feeling.

Foreign Certificate

Use this method for quicker action than URESA. (Be careful: This procedure allows visitation and custody hearings to take place in the county where the non-payor lives. If your children are very young or you have visitation or custody problems, you should consider not using this method.)

Send the following to the Clerk Of Courts where the non-payor lives:

a. Three certified copies of your original order and all changes.

b. Sworn affidavit from you stating the amount of back support owed.

c. Affidavit from your local child support agency which collects and disburses payments stating the amount of back support owed (if possible).

d. Letter from you with your name and address, the children's names and birth dates.

e. Also include the non-payor's address and employment if known. Also include any property, cars, etc. owned if known. Call or write the Clerk Of Courts where the non-payor lives to find out the fee. It is usually under $10. Send a cover letter requesting that the order be registered as a Foreign Certificate To Clerk Of Courts where the non-payor lives.

f. Wait two weeks, then write to the county attorney where the non-payor lives and notify her of Foreign Certificate Registration and ask for enforcement services.

TROUBLE-SHOOTING ON INTERSTATE CASES

"After three unsuccessful years of trying on my own to get action, ACES group action got it done! An income withholding order is in place and may children are receiving regular support payments. The state knew where the non-payor was employed and did nothing, even after the federal laws for mandatory income withholding were in place in all 50 states! ACES taught me how to effectively work as a group to get the government to change for the better."
—M.D., San Bernadino, California

When the state where the non-payor lives does not take action, write the state IV-D agency where you live and where the non-payor lives. If this does not work, contact the Regional IV-D office (see Appendix B).

Call or write the ACES National office. We can assist you by contacting the appropriate agencies and by local ACES chapters working to get local agencies to take actions which assist children.

8. Collecting Child Support From A Self-Employed Non-payor

"My husband quit a perfectly good job with a nice corporation and became self-employed as a 'consultant.' He even told people that he thought that would be an easier way to get away with not paying child support! He was wrong, because I subpoenaed all his records and told him I could get the IRS involved, too. That was enough to get him to comply."

—R.H., Akron, Ohio

COLLECTING CHILD SUPPORT from the self-employed can be difficult. The two major methods available are contempt of court and criminal prosecution. Other civil court remedies include posting a bond by the non-payor, placing the self-employed company in receivership, sequestration of property of the non-payor, placement of liens on property and execution of them.

In contempt of court proceedings ("motion to show cause," "citation"), a motion is filed with the court asking for a hearing to be held to show that the non-payor did not make child support payments as ordered by the court. If a person is found guilty of contempt of court it means that they failed to comply with a court order and the judge can choose to punish them for not following the court order. Being found in contempt of court does not necessarily mean the judge is finding the non-payor to be "wrong" for not supporting their children. It means that the person is being found guilty of not doing what the judge said to do.

Because of this, the judge has control over the punishment of the non-payor for failing to follow the judge's order. He/she can order the person to go to jail until they've "paid up" or paid $500. The judge can order the person to pay $100 in 30 days or go to jail. The judge can also order that the persons post bond to ensure payment, etc. The judge has wide discretion in most states about what they can do to punish a person for contempt of court.

If the judge orders the non-payor to pay $1,000 in 30 days or go to jail at the end of 39 days (if you have not received the payment), you will have to file another motion asking the judge to find the non-payor in contempt of court. Another court hearing is held to determine whether the non-payor complied with the court order. If he did not, at this hearing the judge can put the non-payor in jail or order the non-payor to pay the $1,000 in 30 days or post bond, etc.

Many people end up on a "merry go round" when trying to use contempt of court to enforce child support orders. This occurs when the judge continues to give the non-payor more time to pay up, find a job, etc. Some non-payors will wait until the day of the court hearing to pay the child support because they know that as long as they pay before they have to appear nothing will happen to them. This is a loophole which allows them to not pay child support except when taken to court—about every 60–90 days at most. This means that they can keep the money for themselves longer and collect interest on it.

Contempt of court should not be the first choice of enforcement against anyone, especially a self-employed non-payor, unless you know the judge is a tough enforcer who will impose jail and/or cash bonds.

The judge can order the non-payor to post a bond with the Clerk Of Courts or Child Support Agency to ensure payment of child support. If the payments are missed, they can be withdrawn from the bond money or the court order can say that the entire bond is forfeited upon non-payment. Cash bonds work best in these situations. Surety bonds, also called signature bonds often are not complied with by repeat non-payors. Surety bonds are a promissory note from the non-payor that he/she will make child support payments regularly as ordered by the court. Those with a poor track record at keeping their promises to children rarely keep these promises to the court.

To obtain a finding of contempt of court against a non-payor which will result in a punishment such as time in jail, you will usually need to show the judge evidence that the non-payor had sources of income and failed to support her children. To obtain this evidence there are several methods available.

Subpoena company books, bank accounts records. If these show that the non-payor had income available.

Credit checks. This shows the name of the bank, and loans taken out so that records can be subpoenaed. People list their assets on loan applications. Subpoenaing loan applications are a very good source of obtaining a written list of the non-payors assets. These assets are presented to the judge to prove that the person had the ability to pay support and did not.

You need to prove to the court that payments were not made as ordered by the court. This can be done via an affidavit from the payee (person to whom the payments are to be made), from the certified copy of the arrearage, a record provided by the Clerk of Courts of the Child Support Agency.

Results of a contempt finding can be jail time, a requirement to post a bond, and a lump judgment for the amount of back support which has not been paid. The judgment for the back support can also be used to place a lien on property, attach a bank account, force the sale of a car, motorcycle, recreational vehicle, boat, jewelry, etc. (See Chapter 10 for more detailed information on liens and judgments.)

A judgment can also be used to obtain a writ of sequestration. This is a court order which has been defined as the separation or removal of property from a person for use as decided by the court. In one case, an ACES member was given the non-payors car in exchange for $2,000 in back support due.

Judgment can be used to place liens on property and then foreclosure can occur so that the child support debt can be collected. When one is executing (collecting) a judgment it is important to check various state laws. In some states a house can not be foreclosed upon to collect debts due to Homestead Acts.

The loan on a car, boat, motorcycle, etc. must be paid off out of proceeds from the sale of the vehicle before any of the money can be given to pay off the child support debt. In most states, certain household items such as stoves, refrigerators, about $1,500 in personal property, about $750 in tools, etc., is protected and cannot be taken to pay off a judgment. There is usually a protection on real estate and automobiles. Therefore, the mortgage needs to be almost paid off, the car needs to be new and paid for, and the boat needs not be under a loan from the bank if you wish to "seize" it for collection of the child support debt.

Bank accounts can be taken via an attachment if you have a judgment for child support arrearage. Social Security benefits are attachable, as well as rents received. Almost any source of income or assets are attachable to collect child support once you have a judgment from the court for the arrearage.

The self-employed's company can be placed in a receivership by the court to ensure that child support payments are made. A receivership is when the court appoints a trustee to take over the financial dealings of the company. The trustee is responsible for paying the company's debts and to make sure that payments ordered by the court for child support are paid first.

If the self-employed person has incorporated the business, an income withholding can be used to collect child support. The withholding order would be binding upon the corporation and if the company fails to pay the order, it can be held liable for the amount of child support. The officers of the corporation can be found in contempt of court and placed in jail.

Use of criminal non-support against non-payors who are self-employed or repeat offenders can be very effective. The crime is committed in the state where the child lives. The child must be under age 18 in most states. Criminal non-support means that the parent criminally neglected or abused the child by failing to provide financial support. In some states criminal non-support is a misdemeanor, in other states it is a felony, and in some places non-support is not considered a crime. See list on page one hundred for your state laws.

In a criminal non-support procedure, you will have to show the police department, county or city prosecutor, where you live, that payments have not been made. This can be done by filing a police report, providing an affidavit, or by testifying in front of a grand jury. If the prosecutor or grand jury believes that the crime has occurred, they can obtain a warrant for the arrest of the criminal. The warrant is then served upon the non-payor by the city police or the county sheriff's department and the non-payor is arrested. The non-payor, just like any other criminal, is arraigned and/or released on bond until the trial. Often, non-payors will be released on their own recognizance if they do not have a previous criminal record. At the arraignment the non-payor can plead guilty, not guilty, or no contest to the criminal charges.

If the non-payor pleads guilty, a date is set for sentencing the non-payor. Often, the court will place a first-time offender on probation with the terms of probation being regular child support payments and payments on the arrearage.

If the non-payor pleads no contest it means that they are not admitting their guilt but will take the punishment as deemed appropriate by the court for the crime. A hearing will be set for sentencing on these cases. Usually, as in cases with non-payors who plead guilty, the first-time offender is placed on probation.

If the non-payor pleads not guilty a trial will be held. The non-payor can request a jury trial. At the trial the prosecutor will need to present evidence to the court that the child support payments were not made. The payee will have to testify that payments were not received and the court will need to be provided with a certified copy of an arrearage statement form the Clerk Of Courts or the Child Support Agency. The prosecutor will also need to show the judge that the non-payor had an income during the time they did not make child support payments. The non-payor can be found guilty of non-support if it is proven that he/she had the ability to pay and failed to do so.

In some courts, non-payors who plead guilty to non-support and those found guilty of non-support are placed in work release programs and/or serve time in jail for willfully neglecting their children. People often say that if you put someone in jail you will not be able to collect child support because they are not working. Remind them that work release can be ordered by the court and that placing non-payors on probation with the probation being withdrawn and the non-payor being jailed if payments are missed has proven to be very effective. Studies show that nine out of every ten individuals placed in jail for non-support begin to pay child support.

Use of criminal non-support against those who flee across state lines to avoid paying child support can be effective if your state has laws for felony non-support. Most states will extradite a non-payor on felony non-support. To file these charges and to find out if your case qualifies for felony non-support and extradition, contact your county attorney.

ACES has found that with friendly persuasion, criminal non-support charges and extradition can occur even if it has never happened before in your community, provided state law allows this and you can prove to the county attorney that the non-payor had the ability to pay and willfully failed to support the child.

Apply for IV-D services or request that the court enforce its own order through a contempt hearing. You may hire a private attorney or represent yourself (pro se) in court.

1. Motion is filed for contempt of court hearing. Date is set for court hearing. Hearing takes place:

a. You enter evidence that the non-payor has income: subpoenaed company records, non-payor tax records, and/or present witnesses.

b. Non-payor enters evidence concerning why payment has not been made.

c. Then, you request the court to order:

—That the non-payor is to post a cash bond with the Clerk Of Courts or Child Support Agency (if payments are missed, they are taken from the bond and sent to you), or

—Request a judgment for arrears (must be executed to collect support by placing a lien on a house, car, boat, etc., then forcing sale of the item via foreclosure or sheriff's sale).

Other remedies for non-payment against the self-employed:

1. *Criminal non-support.* File charges at the county attorney's office.

2. *Place the non-payor's company in receivership.* This can be done by a IV-D attorney or a private attorney.

"They actually found the non-payor in contempt of court for refusing to work to support his daughter! All of the struggle was worth it, since now I have taken action to help my daughter!"
—B.B., Portland, Oregon

9. Solving the Most Difficult Problems

"I'm collecting from a man who's just been sent to jail. He's in jail because I wouldn't put my house up to bail him out . . . he's been in trouble for a long time for something unrelated to non-payment of child support. A few years back, he had an accident and is now blind as a result. So, my children are getting a portion of his Social Security payments, but we had to work pretty hard to get them. I garnished his bank account after he was sentenced and got $1,000 from that, too. He still owes more than $25,000 in back support."
—K.R., Council Bluffs, Iowa

Non-payor is unemployed: Unemployment Compensation is attachable for child support under federal law P.L. 97-35. Or, you may ask for a contempt hearing and at the hearing request the court to issue an order that the non-payor is to seek employment and provide proof to the court that he/she is looking for work.

Non-payor is an under-the-table earner: You can request the IV-D agency or private attorney to do a credit check to determine assets. You can request that the court issue you a judgment for back support and then if the non-payor has any assets, you can execute the judgment against a house, car, motorcycle, etc.

Non-payor places assets in someone else's name: Placement of assets (title of car, deed to the house) in someone else's name to avoid a valid debt can be a fraudulent conveyance. The car, house, and bank account can be attached for collection of a valid child support debt if you can prove that the item was transferred to another person after the debt was incurred and the child support payments were missed. You must prove that the non-payor uses the item (drives the car, lives in the house) and prove that the non-payor has value in the item (pays the mortgage or car payment).

Court has issued an order for a money judgment: (See Chapter 7 as well as Chapter 9.)

Non-payor lives out of state and that state is uncooperative: (See Chapter 6.)

Non-payor is self-employed. (See Chapter 7.)

Non-payor is not meeting obligations of court order to pay medical bills or provide medical insurance for the child. You can request a contempt hearing to seek enforcement through IV-D Agency, private attorney, or represent yourself.

Non-payor owes large amount of back support. You can file to attach federal and state income tax refunds if the child is under age 18 at your local IV-D Agency and/or request a judgment from the court and execute the judgment, and/or get payment on back support in addition to current support via a wage withholding.

Non-payor owes alimony in addition to child support. Non-payor owes the welfare department back child support and owes you back support. If you no longer receive AFDC, all current support paid must be given to you by the government child support agency. The back support can be paid to you first to pay off child support arrearages owed to you or it can be used to pay off the AFDC child support debt before you receive it. Also, it could be divided between you and the state for the AFDC child support debt. State laws vary on this issue.

If you currently receive AFDC and child support is collected, you are entitled to receive the first $50 paid in addition to receiving your AFDC check each month. In some states, you may be entitled to more than just $50 of the support. Contact your state Welfare Department and ask them for a copy of the rules about AFDC and child support payments.

If the child support payment is more than the AFDC paid to you each month, you are entitled to receive the child support instead of the AFDC checks. You may still be eligible for food stamps even if you do not receive AFDC and you should be eligible for Medicaid for a year after you stop receiving AFDC.

Attaching Unemployment Compensation

Federal public law (P.L. 97-35), which was passed in 1980, makes it possible to attach an absent parent's Unemployment Compensation benefits for child support.

In order to do this, you must go to the IV-D agency in the state where you live and file an application to attach Unemployment Compensation. Provide them with all the information you have about the absent parent (non-payor's full name, correct address, and Social Security number, if known).

The IV-D Agency is responsible for attaching unemployment compensation for collection of child support. The agency may ask the non-payor to voluntarily sign an attachment, or may have a process to attach the unemployment compensation check administratively or through a court proceeding.

REPEAT OFFENDERS

"He moves between Florida and Alaska, he owns a construction company and hides his assets. When he left the boys and me 15 years ago, we didn't even know where he was for a long time. After he was located, Florida took him into court several times for contempt of court. He hid from the process server to avoid court hearings. When he was finally served, he always seemed to get off scot-free because no

one could find his assets. But the IRS did find his assets; in fact, they closed up his business and sold his cement mixers to collect the $20,000 in back support due. The IRS Full Collection Service worked for me when nothing else did!"

—M.B., Fairlawn, Ohio

The IRS Full Collection Service may be the answer to problems of collecting support from repeat offenders, self-employed, and/or out-of-state non-payors. If you are owed at least $750 in back support and other methods to collect it have been tried without success, the non-payor's seizable assets can be collected by the IRS in the same manner they use to collect back taxes.

Special action can be taken to help in a case where the non-payor has a history of non-support.

1. The court can order the posting of a cash bond to ensure payment.

2. The court can order the business of a self-employed non-payor to be placed in receivership. The receiver then allocates income to ensure support obligation is met.

3. A special procedure is available through the IV-D Agency if children are under age 18. The IRS Full Collection Service can be used on very difficult cases with large arrearages over $750. ACES' procedure is recommended to be used for the self-employed and out-of-state cases with arrearages over $5,000. The non-payor must have attachable assets.

Procedure

1. File IV-D application with the local agency.

2. Request IRS full collection services in writing to local, state, and regional IV-D Agency. (See Appendix for list.)

3. Get approval from the local, state, and regional IV-D offices. This is a step you **must** follow.

4. IRS then handles the case the same way back taxes are collected, including shutting down a business, seizure of all property, and jail terms.

GETTING THE IRS TO
HELP YOU COLLECT CHILD SUPPORT

Attaching federal and state income tax refunds for collection of back support is one way to collect "large" portions of back child support owed to your children. Over a billion dollars of back support has been collected through the IRS Offset Program since it began in 1980.

The program was expanded to include families not receiving AFDC benefits in 1985. ACES is requesting that the program be expanded to include collections of child support for families where the children are over age 18, and that child support be moved up in the priority system.

Currently, IRS tax refunds are attached first for back taxes, second for outstanding federal student loans, and then for child support. ACES would like to see child support collections placed before student loans.

To qualify for an attachment of a federal and/or state income tax refund:

1. You must have a court order for child support.

2. You must be owed at least $500 in back support if you do not receive AFDC or you must be owed at least $150 if you receive AFDC.

3. You must have a IV-D case. This means that you have filled out an application at your local child support enforcement agency. (See Appendix for a list of state IV-D agencies.)

The Child Support Enforcement Agency should:

1. Verify that you are owed back child support. They can do this by contacting the agency or Clerk of Courts which receives payments on your case, or they can have you sign a notarized statement which lists the amount of back support you are owed.

2. The Social Security number of the non-payor must be known by you or the Child Support Enforcement Agency.

3. The Child Support Enforcement Agency can require you to sign a special application for the IRS Offset or it can be included in your IV-D application. You need to contact the child support agency to find out if you need to fill out a special application. In states where a special application is required, you need to do this in June or July of each year to attach the following year's income tax refund.

ISSUES YOU SHOULD BE AWARE OF CONCERNING THE IRS

1. A non-payor or their current spouse can file an amended income tax return for up to six years after the original is filed. If this is done and the non-payor and/or the current spouse should not have received all or part of the refund and it has been passed onto you, the money will have to be paid back by you. In ACES' experience, this rarely occurs, since most people only amend income tax refunds to obtain more of a refund rather than to pay additional.

2. Injured spouse provisions: This program has special provisions to allow the current spouse of a non-payor to claim their part of the income tax refund. The child support agency can hold the monies attached for up to six months to allow the current spouse to file a claim for their portion of the income tax refund. (If you live in a state with a divorce community property law this does not apply.) If the spouse files a legitimate claim you may have to pay the money back to the Child Support Enforcement Agency who by law must refund the money to the current spouse. In ACES' experience, claims by the current spouse frequently occur, so be sure to find out if any of the money you receive belongs to the current spouse before you spend it! You can do this by directly contacting the non-payor's spouse or by having the child support agency do it for you.

3. If you have ever received AFDC benefits and there is

back child support owed to the state, they have "first dibs" on the child support collected from the attachment of the income tax refund. This is a good, quick, painless way to get the state "paid off."

For Your Information

The income tax return will be taken in the spring of the year and it can be held for up to six months to give the non-payor time to file an appeal about the tax return being taken. The non-payor can file an amended tax return for up to three years after the money is given to you. You can be held responsible to return the money to the Child Support Agency.

If you have been an AFDC case in the past and the non-payor owes money to the welfare department, the welfare department will get their money from the income tax return before you receive your back support.

The Child Support Agency can refuse your request to attach the income tax return if:

1. You have not filled out an application for child support services.

2. You are not owed $500 for no less than three months.

3. You refuse to sign an affidavit.

Under-the-table Earners

Under-the-table-earners are those who receive pay in cash or through some hidden source.

These enforcement methods are available:

1. *Credit check.* Local IV-D agency or private attorney can provide this service. Credit check could show hidden assets.

2. *Criminal non-support charges* can be filed for refusal to work if non-payor quits job when wage withholding is implemented, etc. They cannot be used if non-payor receives welfare benefits. File charge with county attorney. Requirements and punishments vary from state to state.

3. *Contempt of court hearing* can be held. The judge can order

non-payor to seek work and report to the court with proof that he/she is seeking employment. If non-payor fails to provide proof that he/she is seeking employment he/she can then be sent to jail after the second contempt hearing is held.

10. Seizing Assets And Other Methods of Collecting Back Support

"I didn't give up on my local support agency. We found a legal way to attach an insurance settlement of his. I wound up with $12,000 in back support!"

—K.T. ACES of Ohio

FINDING OUT THE income and property owned by a non-payor is essential to successful child support enforcement. It is especially important if the non-payor is self-employed or earns money under-the-table.

You will need to answer these questions as completely as possible:

1. Absent parent's current employer, salary, pay periods.

2. Commissions and bonuses received.

3. Deductions from pay such as savings plans, credit union accounts, etc.

4. Property owned by absent parent—check with county deed office.

5. Rents received.

6. Bank accounts—name, address, account number.

7. Stock owned.

8. Lawsuits absent parent has pending which will produce income such as inheritance, personal injury, work-related claims.

9. Motor vehicles, boats, motorcycles, etc., owned by absent parent. Check with the State Department of Motor Vehicles for license numbers.

10. Private, military, or government benefits received such as pension, disability, etc. Personal property such as jewelry, art collections or coin collections.

12. Professional licenses owned by absent parent.

OTHER METHODS TO
DETERMINE ASSETS OF ABSENT PARENTS

1. Deposition/Discovery: Absent parent is questioned under oath by your attorney or IV-D attorney.

2. Information from employers can be obtained by attorneys contacting the company, or you or your attorney can subpoena the employer for a court hearing.

3. A credit bureau check can determine assets. This can be done by the IV-D attorney or a private attorney.

4. Bank records, tax returns, and financial records of a company can be subpoenaed into court.

5. IV-D agency can check federal tax form 1099 to determine assets such as stocks, bonds, and interest (Project 412). You can obtain a judgment issued by the court. However, a judgment will only provide child support payments if it is executed. The non-payor has the option to voluntarily.

To execute a judgment, the non-payor must have assets such as:

1. Property (house, land).

2. Car (usually valued at $1,000 or more).

3. Boat, motorcycle, etc.

4. Jewelry, art work, etc.

5. Bank accounts, stocks, bonds,

6. Certificates of deposit (CDs),

7. Commissions, bonuses, vacation pay.

Usually, if not always, you will need an attorney to execute a judgment, since it is a very technical legal process. Sometimes attorneys will take a case on a contingency basis such as 20–30% of what you collect. IV-D attorneys can also execute judgments.

Other Assets to Check

1. Unemployment compensation is attachable by local IV-D agency.

2. Worker's compensation is attachable in some states.

3. Social Security benefits received by an absent parent may mean your child is eligible for benefits. Check with your local Social Security office. Also, Social Security is attachable to collect child support.

4. Military benefits are attachable (contact ACES for military benefit attachment packet).

5. V.A. benefits received by an absent parent may provide an allotment for the child.

6. Trust income is attachable.

7. Inheritance is attachable.

Please remember: You must be persistent in your investigation to be successful. Many children have received the support they deserve only after the custodial parent got enough information to provide evidence in court that the non-payor truly did have assets!

Liens/Judgments

"I was able to garnish the money in his savings account in the U.S. after he moved to Brazil because the court issued a judgment which said I could. That helped collect some of the back support."
—K.R., Council Bluffs, Iowa

JUDGMENTS

1. You can obtain a judgment for back child support through a court proceeding. A IV-D attorney or a private attorney can represent you at the hearing, or you can represent yourself (pro se). You should request that the judgment include interest on arrears (back support).

2. The judgment must then be executed to collect money due. (See Chapter 7 in addition to the following information.)

LIENS

First you must perfect the lien by filing the judgment with the Clerk Of Courts.

The duration of a lien varies from state to state. For example, if you place a lien on a house and do not foreclose, you will have to rejuvenate the lien about every 5–10 years, or it becomes useless.

Priority status of a lien is usually that the first lien gets the first money, second lien gets second money, etc.

Property affected by liens includes:

a. Real property—home, land.
b. Personal property—jewelry, artwork, coin collections, etc.
c. Motor vehicles (usually must be worth more than $1,000).
d. Boats, motorcycles and recreational vehicles.

Enforcement of Liens

Laws vary from state to state. You will probably need an attorney to enforce the lien, or the IV-D attorney can assist you (see the No-Nonsense Legal Guide, *How to Choose a Lawyer,* for more information on obtaining counsel).

Other Methods Of Enforcement On Judgments

1. *Writ of execution (fiera facias) (levy)*: Sheriff seizes property and it is placed for public sale. The cost of court fees and appraisal will be deducted from the monies collected. The reminder of funds should go toward your judgment. IV-D attorneys, private attorneys or pro se actions can accomplish this.

2. *Garnishment; Writ of garnishment*: Non-payor is notified—if no defense is presented, the employer is notified and wages are taken. Garnishments must be done against each pay check. Income withholdings are done automatically on each pay check.

3. *Creditors bill*: Purpose is to force non-payor to turn over assets to the court for child support debt.

4. *Foreclosure*: Forced sale of real or personal property.

11. Be All that You Can Be

Collecting From Military Personnel

"I finally started collecting back and current support because I wrote a letter to his commanding officer. I even enclosed pictures of the kids! Once his C.O. found out that he owed support, his wages were withheld and my children began to see some money."
— S.H., Zanesville, Ohio

ALL U.S. MILITARY personnel have a regulatory obligation to support dependents.

You can collect from military personnel by contacting the commanding officer of the non-payor. Write a letter, and include a copy of your court order (certified if possible); state your name and address, and length of time child support has not been paid. The non-payor's name and service number should also be included, if known.

Remind the commanding officer that the non-payor has broken a military regulation and should be counseled. If the commanding officer is sympathetic to you, he or she can order the serviceman to pay the obligation. If the commanding officer doesn't help you, you can do an involuntary garnishment.

HOW TO FIND MILITARY PERSONNEL

To find a person in the military, contact the appropriate military locator:

Army (317) 542-4211
Navy (202) 694-3155
Coast Guard (202) 426-8898
Air Force (512) 652-5774
Marines (202) 694-1624

If a serviceman is 60 days behind in support payments, you can obtain an involuntary allotment. (Alimony, too, if there is a child support order). This requires that a withholding order be sent to the military. The IV-D Agency or Child Support Enforcement Agency can assist you with this procedure. The total time to collect should be within 60 days after the military receives the order.

To accomplish the sending of the withholding order, apply to be a IV-D case at your local child support agency. You must:

1. Be owed two months' support and send an affidavit or certified copy of arrears from Clerk Of Courts or IV-D Agency.

2. Have the service member's full name and social security number.

3. Include your name and address.

4. Send entire package *via registered mail* to proper military branch.

The addresses and phone numbers of the military offices are as follows:

Unites States Army
Commander
United States Army
Finance & Accounting Center
Attn: FINCL
Indianapolis, IN 46249
(317) 542-2155
(317) 542-2154

United States Air Force
Air Force Academy Finance Center
Attn: RPT
Denver, CO 80279-5000
(303) 370-7051

United States Navy

Navy Finance Center
Retired Pay Department Code
301
1240 East 9th Street
Cleveland, OH 44199-2058
(216) 522-5630

United States Marine Corps

Marine Corps Finance Center
Code CPR
Kansas City, MO 64197-0001
1(800) 645-2024

United States Coast Guard

Commanding Officer
U.S. Coast Guard Pay & Personnel Center
444 Southeast Quincy Street
Topeka, KS 66683
(913) 295-2657

To collect support from a military member when you do not have a court order, write to the commanding officer, who may order the service person to arrange for payment. Establish paternity, if necessary. The IV-D child support agency can do this for you for a maximum $25 fee.

A hearing may then be held, during which time an attorney may be appointed for the service member if he or she does not attend or send an attorney. (Note: Make sure an attorney is appointed for the service member if needed. *Do not* let the case get dropped because he or she "no-shows.")

Medical Benefits

To collect medical benefits for children of military personnel, contact the commanding officer and requesting help in securing CHAMPUS (Civilian Health and Medical Program of the Uniformed Services) coverage for the children. The service member must enroll in DEERS (Defense Enrollment Eligibility Reporting System) for dependents to get medical coverage. Or, contact your closest military installation. Supply them with copies of the childrens' birth certificates and information about the service person. They can arrange for CHAMPUS and DEERS.

But How Much Does He/She Make?

To determine the amount of income of the military service member, contact your local recruiting office and obtain the

following: a Monthly Basic Pay Schedule (which lists classi-
fication and pay rate), Basic Allowance for Quarters, and
Variable Housing Allowance. Service members receive additional allowances for dependents. This can be used to determine the amount of support that should be paid by applying
the income to the child support guidelines.

PART V

OTHER ISSUES

12. Obtaining Medical Support For Children

"After I found out that he got a new job (after several months of unemployment), I got the judge to attach his wages and get the kids on his medical insurance. Now I don't have to worry about them in case they get sick."

—M.N., Boston, Massachusetts

YOU HAVE A right to obtain a court order for medical support of your children from the non–custodial parent. This court order can be part of your divorce decree or separation order.

If your current court order does not have a requirement for medical insurance for the children, arrangements for payment of medical bills, or you do not have a court order of any type, you can get one by:

1. Contacting the local/state child support agency IV–D agency. Complete an application at the child support agency and write on the application that you want medical support in addition to child support payments;

2. You can hire a private attorney, if you wish, to obtain a medical support order;

3. Or you can represent yourself (pro se).

Suggested items to have included in your medical support order:

1. A requirement that you are to be provided annually,

signed insurance claim forms, insurance identification cards and policy numbers (if the non-custodial parent is to have health insurance for the child).

2. Immediate notice to you by the non-custodial parent if the insurance lapses for any reason.

3. A specific listing of how bills are to be paid if not covered by the medical insurance (if none is available to either parent or insurance pays only part of the bills).

If the medical insurance pays 80% of medical bills, the remaining 20% will be evenly divided between the parents or paid in full by the non-custodial parent, or paid 20% by the custodial parent and 80% by the non-custodial parent, etc.

GETTING THE CHILD SUPPORT AGENCY TO HELP

Federal laws US 662(b) and US 654(4)(b) require state/local child support agencies to obtain medical support orders if the non-custodial parent has health insurance available to him/her from his/her employer, for the children.

They are also required to enforce this, but they are not required to help you collect unpaid medical bills not covered by insurance or bills that occurred due to the non-custodial parent not having health insurance when it was part of the court order to do so.

The child support agency should file a motion with the court requesting establishment of a medical support order. There will be a court hearing and you will be represented by an attorney from the Child Support Agency. It is best if you can attend the court hearing to make sure that the attorney tells your side of the story in full.

If you have an order that the non-custodial parent is to have health insurance and he/she has ignored the order, the Child Support Agency should file a motion with the court asking that the non-compliant parent be found in contempt. This is often called a "motion to show cause."

There will be a court hearing to determine if the non-compliant parent has good reason not to have the children covered under his/her health insurance. If good reason is not found by the court, the non-complaint parent should be ordered by the court to place the children on his/her health insurance policy.

You should request that the court place a specific date in the court order for the non-compliant parent to meet, and it should also state that there is some type of punishment if the parent continues to ignore the court order, such as a fine or jail time. This is usually needed, since the parent has been told in the past to put the children on the health insurance policy and has failed to do so.

HOW TO COLLECT BACK MEDICAL SUPPORT

There is no current federal requirement for the Child Support Agency to help you collect past-due medical bills, although some states provide this service. Check with the Child Support Agency in your state. If you live in a state which does not provide this service, you can represent yourself in court or hire a private attorney to collect the past-due bills.

If you obtain a "lump sum" judgment from the court for the amount of medical bills (a court order which states that the parent owes the bills and lists a specific amount owed), the state/local child support agency must collect on the judgment for you.

If you choose to represent yourself in court, you will need to file a motion with the court. (See Appendix for Sample Motion.) In some counties, the Clerk Of Courts has pre-made forms you can use. In other places, you must make your own forms. Check the local library's legal section to see samples of forms used in your community.

Type the forms or use a pre-printed form.

Take the form to the Clerk Of Courts and file it. There is

usually a small fee, or if you cannot afford the filing fee, give the Clerk's office a notarized statement that you are poverty level or below (this is called an "affidavit of poverty").

At the hearing, have your medical bills well-organized. The court will want to see the original bills received from the doctors, hospitals, etc. In addition to bringing the medical bills to court, make a written list which includes the child's name, amount due, name of health care provider and amount paid by insurance.

You will need copies of the bills and the list to give to the non-custodial parent, his/her attorney, and a copy for yourself. Give the court the original bills and the list of pertinent information mentioned above.

Be sure to ask the court specifically for what you want. Here's an example: "I want Bob X. to pay this bill in full in 30 days, or to increase child support payments to pay off medical bills, or a judgment for the amount due."

Things To Know If You Hire a Private Attorney

Remember that the attorney works for you. Tell him/her exactly what you want to accomplish. If the attorney suggests that you can accept an offer from the non-custodial parent's attorney or from him/her, ask yourself:

1. Will this make sure that my children get health care?

2. Will this make sure that there is a way for me to actually collect the money due?

3. Will this make sure that my children have received all that they are due?

If you make an agreement with the non-custodial parent and/or his/her attorney, you cannot appeal the decision to the court. This is called an "agreed court order."

If you are not satisfied with the "deal," you can request a full court hearing. If you don't agree with the court order, you may have the right to appeal the judge's (or hearing officer's, referee's, master's, etc.) order.

13. What To Tell The Kids

"The children worry about being evicted and the electricity being shut off. I try to hide these worries from them, but it is almost impossible. It does not seem fair that their joy of childhood is being lost. I am angry about the situation and worried about the children's futures."

—K.T., Swanton, Ohio

IT IS ALMOST impossible to protect the children from the daily strain caused by lack of money to pay bills and meet obligations. It is even more difficult for the children when whatever they ask for they cannot be given.

Some of the worst memories are Christmases with little or nothing under the tree, and having to say, "No, I can't buy you that Mickey Mouse beachball." It seems, many times, like you're always the one saying, "No."

Children can develop a negative relationship with the custodial parent because of these problems. Having an open and honest relationship is paramount. This is the only way you can explain why there is no extra money right now and to explain what child support payments are and why your family needs them.

This really needs to be done in a matter-of-fact manner so that it doesn't frighten the child or cause the children to blame themselves for the problems.

If children hear constant complaints about not receiving child support payments and the high cost of raising children, it may make them feel like a burden to you—and also may cause them to feel unwanted. You need to gently explain that both parents are responsible for supporting children and that it is right to pursue collection of support.

Children should not be part of preparations for court hearings. They do not need to be part of discussions where you vent your anger or frustrations about the problems associated with collecting child support. Protecting the children from these types of discussions will help ensure that they feel safe and secure and that it is acceptable to love both parents.

Children have the capability of loving both parents without loving one less. They have the capability of determining which parent is unselfish and which is not. They will and can learn this through association with both parents better than any other influence.

It is tempting to tell children that the other parent doesn't care about them or love them because they don't care enough to send money or food. However, this may only make the child feel self-blame or self-anger, rather than anger towards the non-payor.

To help children cope after divorce/separation:

1. Reassure them it's not their fault.

2. Don't criticize the other parent in front of the child. If you cannot say positive things about the other parent, limit what you say in front of the child to "just the facts."

3. Don't blame the child's fears, behavior, or any other problem on the other parent, the divorce, the separation, or lack of child support.

4. Let the child know it is okay to love both parents and to want to be like either Mom or Dad.

5. Don't turn your child into a "confidant." Your child is not an adult and can't handle the full burdens of adult problems and decisions.

6. Don't use your child as a messenger between you and your ex-spouse, or use the child as a pawn in an unresolved "divorce war."

7. Don't put words into your child's mouth. For example, don't turn "Daddy got a new car" into "Daddy bought a $25,000 car and he doesn't pay enough child support."

8. Don't pump the child for information about your ex-spouse.

9. Don't use the child as a spy.

10. Protect the child from being a direct part of actions to enforce a court order, such as the court hearing, arrest of a non-payor, etc. If the activity will be public, it is better that you tell the child in a calm and positive manner rather than have the child hear about the arrest from a neighbor or a friend.

Remember, children follow your lead. If you fall apart (and because you're human, you will sometimes), so will they. It's okay—just cry for a while, then get back on track. They will follow your lead.

It is okay for the children to know that you're angry about child support, as long as you let them know that it is okay for them to have their feelings, too. In fact, it is okay to not be perfect, to not always handle everything. If you are having problems coping as a parent or single parent, seek out support groups such as a local chapter of ACES or Parents Without Partners. Or contact a private counselor if that would make you feel more comfortable.

Going through tough times as a family can lead to a closer, more loving family—or it can be totally destructive. So, take positive action as early as you can for your children. Above all, be fair and honest—with them and yourself.

14. Guess Who's Coming To Dinner?

Visitation/Custody Issues

"I was initially hesitant to allow my ex visitations rights, mainly because he was verbally abusive. I told the judge this, and my ex agreed to supervised visitation. That way, he can still see his son and I don't have to worry as much."

—H.M., Billings, Montana

ALMOST ALL COURT orders from a divorce, dissolution, establishment of paternity, or separation order include a provision for visitation or companionship. There are several types of visitation orders. Here are some samples:

a. Visitation as agreed to by both partners.
b. Reasonable visitation.
c. Court-scheduled visitation.
d. A specific time table may be listed in your decree.

General Visitation orders. Court orders which state only "reasonable visitation" give the custodial parent broad discretion and the decision-making powers about when visitation will occur. Visitation "as agreed to by both parties" offers parents an opportunity to build a mutually acceptable flexible schedule for visitation. This type of order works well if you have a good relationship with you ex-spouse.

General visitation orders can cause problems if you and your ex-spouse are having difficulty agreeing which activities the child may participate in; for instance, you may not like your son to play football, but his father may not mind. Such difficulties should be worked out ahead of time—preferably not in front of the child.

Specific visitation orders (court-scheduled). An order which specifies the exact days and times of visitation often helps resolve arguments over what is reasonable. The court sets up the ground rules and offers families an opportunity to know in advance what the schedule will be. These court rules carry the same weight as a state law and are binding on families if they are in your order.

A specific court order for visitation can include information about the following issues:

Cost of transportation for visitation. The order might say that the cost of air fare for the child should be paid for by the non-custodial parent, the custodial parent, or divided between the parents.

Period of time. The order might say the child is to be with the non-custodial parent during summer vacation, spring vacation and/or a week at Christmas or Easter. Often the order lists every other weekend and one evening per week as visitation times.

Health and safety issues. These may be listed in the order as well, and often include items such as the non-custodial parent must provide a car seat to transport the child in; must ensure that the child receives needed medication, special diet foods, etc.

Any other issues in the child's best interest may be included in the order. Issues the judge can be requested to consider might be prior involvement of each parent with the child; what to do about missed visitation; available time of the child, of parent(s), school schedule, distance to travel for visit, age of the child, desires of the child, time spent with siblings, and other issues related to the child's best interests.

Termination of companionship can usually only be accomplished if you can prove physical endangerment of the child by the non-custodial parent.

The court can then issue an order to terminate companionship. Supervised companionship/visitation can be ordered by the court if the non-custodial parent is proven not to be protecting the child's physical and emotional well-being during visitation. Reasons to request a court order for supervised visitation include:

1. Safety of the child (car seats, environmental needs, etc.).
2. Protection from physical abuse.
3. Protection from exposure to alcohol and drug abuse.
4. Protection from emotional abuse.
5. History of domestic violence in the family.

RESOLVING PROBLEMS WITH VISITATION

A specific timetable is the best type of court order to have if you are encountering problems, because it specifically states the rules (example: child must be picked up 7 P.M. on Friday and return home by 6 P.M. Sunday).

If you do not have a specific visitation court order and you are having problems, you can modify or change your order so that it lists a specific schedule. This can be done by filing a motion with the court in the county where the original order was issued, or in the county where the child lives.

To change a visitation order, you can file the papers yourself ("pro se"). You can contact the courts for assistance. In some states, free attorneys may be provided to help you. You can also contact the local Bar Association or obtain an attorney from the "pro bono" (free) attorney program if you are low-income.

You can request that the court issue an order that specifies the dates and times for visitation, lists who is responsible for the child, and a requirement that both parents keep each other informed of addresses and phone numbers the child may be reached at. Where there are severe problems, including a requirement for a visitation itinerary may alleviate some problems.

If you can, go to court and ask for your order to be changed to a supervised visitation order if you already have a specific schedule outlined in your order and you are still having problems. For example, if the non-custodial parent places the child in danger by taking him or her to unfavorable environments, ask the court to change the order to supervised visitation or to suspend visitation altogether until the parent seeks counselling or changes the undesirable behavior.

You will have to prove that the parent endangered the child during visitation. Merely telling the court that the non-custodial parent takes the child to a bar, etc., is not sufficient evidence, especially if you have no witnesses.

To build a winning case, show the court that you are willing to provide the other parent visitation opportunities as long as the child is safe and well taken care of.

You can prove that the child has not been adequately cared for by:

Contacting witnesses. It's best if these are not relatives. A clergyman or community social worker is best.

Written evidence. A statement should say that you have attempted to resolve the problem by writing your ex-spouse and asking him or her to correct the problems to no avail. This shows the judge that you are reasonable and willing to work with the other parent as long as the child is safe. Use the letter in conjunction with a witness who can testify that the child was taken into a bar, or was present when drugs were being used, etc. Show the court any proof of prior violations of the law, if proof exist.

Supervised Visitation This type of court order requires the child and the non-custodial parent to be with another responsible adult during visitation. Often, this is a grandparent, a social worker, or clergy. Judges often order this type of visitation when the non-custodial parent has been found guilty of child abuse, drunk driving, or has participated in any other type of crime.

All states have laws to protect children from physical abuse. If a parent has been found guilty of abusing the child, the judge can suspend visitation until the parent seeks treatment and proves him or herself fit. Or, visitation can be permanently terminated.

If the non-custodial parent has not seen the child in a long period of time, you can show the court that you are willing to work to gradually re-establish the parent-child relationship by asking for a supervised visitation order. This allows the child some time in a safe environment to get to know the non-custodial parent again. Once the relationship is re-established, the court will allow visitation to occur in a more "normal" fashion.

If there have been many visitation problems in the past, the child may be confused or upset. A gradual rescheduling will help the child to adjust. (For example, Sunday afternoons for one month, then all day Saturday or Sunday for a month, progressing to overnight visitation.)

Re-establishing a relationship can take time and energy, but it is well worth the trouble.

Above all else, don't deny visitation out of anger. If there is a problem, take the case back to court!

If you willfully deny a responsible non-custodial parent visitation, you can be charged with and possibly found guilty of contempt of court. Contempt charges against you are a civil court action and punishments are usually left to the discretion of the court. Parents who willfully deny visitation can be sent to jail, or can be warned that if they continue to interfere with the visitation order, they can be sent to jail.

If you are having continued problems involving visitation and your child has been caught in the middle for an extended period of time, consider asking the court for court-ordered counseling for the child and both parents. Try to make a plan that is agreeable to both parents and the child.

Tips on Visitation

★ Remember, children have the capacity to love both parents: They will settle into an acceptable relationship with both if they are safe and loved.

★ Be home when the child is supposed to be picked up, or call the other parent if you will be late.

★ Send dress clothes, play clothes, and favorite toys with the child. This helps the child to feel secure in a different environment.

★ Be at home when the child is scheduled to return or call the other parent if you will be late.

★ Try to make the time with the non-custodial parent as "normal" as possible. Don't make it into a big deal.

★ Work with the other parent to make all possible attempts to keep the child on schedule: feeding time for infants, nap time, participation in activities, etc.

★ Ask the other parent to let you know if the child will be doing something other than the routine. Ask to be provided with information about how to reach the parent and the child, if necessary.

★ Don't interfere between the child and the other parent. Allow their relationship to grow in a natural way. Don't phone the child unless the visitation is longer than normal or the child has a special need. Ask the other parent to allow the child to call you if he or she wishes to.

★ Don't ask the child lots of questions about the other parent; don't use the child as a messenger or a spy.

Visitation And Teenagers

Teenagers frequently do not wish to spend time with either parent. They would much rather be with their friends. If you attempt to arrange visitation around their schedule so they can attend school dances, dates, sports events, etc., they will be much more apt to be cooperative and therefore enjoy time spent with either parent. If possible, involve the teenager in the planning of the visits. Direct communication between the non-custodial parent and the teenager is helpful.

Out Of County Or Out Of State Visitation

In most cases, the distance that the child must travel makes it impossible to follow a regular every-other-weekend or every-other-weekday evening schedule.

Try to get a schedule that fits into the child's school or social activities. School vacation time works well for this, as does every other holiday and an extended time period during the summer.

Children under age five are too young to travel alone via airlines. The airlines require that they be accompanied in case the child develops a fear of flying and will be resistive to traveling long distances alone. Be sure to let the court know if your child is expressing any such fear. Ask the court to require the non-custodial parent to arrange for an adult to fly with the child.

A Final Note

In a recent study of time spent by school-age children with custodial parents who work full time, it was found that there are about 15 quality hours per week. The quality time spent by the non-custodial parent (who visits regularly) and the child was 12 hours per week. This is based on an every-other-week schedule. This study includes time spent with focused attention on your child. Your time with your child is important and your child needs you to be a good role model. Show the child that you are putting his or her needs first.

If the non-custodial parent is a positive role model, encourage contact with the child. Tell the parent he or she may write letters, call on the phone, or contact the school to arrange the receiving of PTA announcements, report cards, and a list of school activities. All public schools receive federal funding and must comply with the parent's request.

If there is high tension between you and the other parent, avoid confrontations at events where the child is present. Be polite; you don't have to have long conversations or discussions.

15. Effective Complaining

Getting the System To Take Action On Your Case

"$20,000 in back support was finally collected. The non-payor had been working at a full-time job with a utility company; for all of seven years he failed to support his children. A URESA from Ohio to Illinois produced absolutely no results. I learned from ACES how to get the government child support agency to move on my case. I complained to the State Child Support Agency and the Federal Office of Child Support, and it worked!"

—J.B., Alton, Illinois

DOES YOUR CASEWORKER fail to return your phone calls? Does your caseworker tell you it is hopeless—to give up? Does your caseworker tell you that you don't qualify for all the things you have heard that can be done to collect on your case? Have you applied for assistance from the local Child Support Enforcement Agency only to never hear from them again?

If your answer is yes to any of the questions above, unfortunately you are not alone. The federal Office of Child Support reports that collections were made on only 10% of the Child Support IV-D cases in 1986. There is not 90% unemployment, nor are 90% of the child support cases in the U.S. uncollectible.

The problems are bureaucracy and the attitude among some workers to "write off" the "tough cases."

If you have not had any action taken on your case for over six months, the odds are that your case is stacked in a pile of papers labeled "dead cases."

It's time to raise your case from the dead! Only you can do it. Your children deserve support and have only you to fight for them. Yes, it is a hassle and a confrontation that all of us would rather avoid. But avoiding the problem only makes dead files get bigger and causes more children to live in poverty.

Take action now—you can do it!!

Follow the chain of command at your local Child Support Agency, both within your state and the nation. By following the chain of command, no agency along the way can say, "We would have helped if you had just asked."

Step 1. Request on the phone or in person what you want done by your caseworker.

Step 2. Complain to the caseworker's supervisor in writing if no action is taken.

Step 3. Complain to the director of the agency in writing if no action is taken.

Step 4. Complain to the State IV-D Agency and the Regional IV-D Agency in writing.

Step 5. Complain to the federal Office of Child Support in Washington, D.C., 370 L'Enfant Promenade SW, Washington, DC 20447.

Contacting ACES Can Help, Too

Complaints work best if your local ACES Chapter is aware of the problem and can include your problem when they discuss issues with the IV-D agencies. If you have no local chapter in your area, consider starting one. Also, the ACES National Office will assist you and is available for you by telephone or written correspondence.

The important thing to remember is that you don't have to fight this problem alone. ACES members are available to support you; all that is asked is that you reach out and help other ACES members in their struggle!

Rules For Winning a Court Case

1. Know your legal rights—attend ACES chapter meetings or contact ACES' National Office.

2. File correct motions; include requests for what you want.

3. Have proof ready to show that the non-payor has a source of income and did not pay child support.

4. Talk to your attorney from the Child Support Agency or your private attorney. Tell them precisely what you want done. Remember, you are the boss and paying them, either personally or through your tax dollars.

5. Go to the hearing if possible. It is not necessary if it is out-of-state, but you should write and call the attorney in the other state. Send pictures of the children so that the attorney knows you and your children are real, not just pieces of paper.

6. Make sure you receive a copy of your court order and READ IT! File an appeal if you are not satisfied. This is the only way to stop "bad court orders from being real." If you are represented by the local Child Support Agency, they can file the appeal for you.

For More Information

For information about how to contact the ACES Chapter closest to you, call ACES' toll-free number: 1(800)537–7072.

Summary

"Unbelievable—I couldn't have done it without ACES! A $3,000 check for part of the back support owed to my daughter was given to us last week. I am glad that I am an ACES member! With ACES' help, I can make sure my daughter receives all the support she is due."

—D.F., Chicago, Illinois

HOW DID WE GET HERE?

THIS IS A question I have asked myself many times in the past six years as ACES has grown. I know that I got here because my sons, Matt and Jake, did not receive child support payments to which they were entitled for more than seven years. I was frustrated that a sluggish bureaucratic child support enforcement system failed to help my children collect their payments.

I was tired and angry when nothing happened every time I contacted my local child support agency for help.

Like many other issues of prime importance to society, nothing is done until the victims themselves unite for action. ACES arose from these same impulses. We grew from a nucleus of women who had "been there."

We had experienced poverty. We had made choices each day which were difficult and sometimes wrong. We struggled as single parents. Most of us had circumstances that put us on welfare.

Some of us had become dependent on other men, since society teaches us that we cannot make it alone. Often, we found out that these new relationships were damaging to us and our children.

Some of us had problems coping with the everyday stresses of single-parenting and turned to alcohol and other addictions to help us cope, only to find that these caused life to become worse—not better.

All of us wanted what was best for our children and worked towards that goal every day. Often we felt that the goal moved farther away rather than closer with each effort we made.

Luckily, we found each other and began to build an organization to help us take better care of our children. We have been successful. All ACES leaders throughout the nation share in the fact that we have made a difference for many families.

Now, when those entitled to child support feel helpless and hopeless, when they have financial problems caused by non-support surround them, they have us to turn to for help.

I often think of ACES as a group of people who have made it through a nightmare and are now reaching back to pull others out of it, too.

Please don't give up on your case—and when you finally do succeed, try to help others by joining ACES.

APPENDIX

Appendix A
More About ACES

ACES, a non-profit national organization, provides the following literature concerning children's rights:
—Child Support Enforcement.
—Establishment of Paternity.
—Visitation.
—Positive Single Parenting.
—Divorce/dissolution.
—Personal/telephone counseling and monthly meetings for problem solving and discussion are available and open to the public.

The programs that ACES provides empower parents to enforce and/or establish child support court orders, provide advocacy with local, state, and federal public officials who are responsible for child support enforcement, and increase public awareness concerning the plight of affected families.

ACES representatives are members of the Ohio Domestic Relations Task Force, Michigan Child Support Guideline Committee, Texas Child Support Guideline Committee, Nevada Commission of Child Support, Alabama Child Support Task Force, Oregon Child Support Guideline Committee, Missouri Child Support Commission, North Dakota Child Support Guidelines Committee, and the Ohio/Kentucky Interstate Child Support Task Force.

For the past five years, ACES has sponsored a national candelight vigil to "Light A Spark Of Hope For Forgotten Children." ACES members in all 50 states participate. Fifteen states issued proclamations for Child Support Day, and several cities issued proclamations. Event speakers included members of Congress, judges, representatives of the federal Office Of Child Support, state and local officials.

The organization receives technical assistance from Advocates for Basic Legal Equality, Inc. (ABLE), and the Center for Law and Social Policy, and various social services agencies.

ACES Chapters meet monthly with local public officials for discussion and problem solving. State Boards meet regularly with state officials, and ACES' National Board of trustees advocate with federal officials concerning child support issues. ACES' national office, located in Toledo, Ohio, provides an information "hot-line" for families in need throughout the United States and provided more than 100,000 families with telephone assistance and/or informational mailings since 1985.

NATIONAL ATTENTION

ACES has been featured in *Parent's* magazine, *Good Housekeeping*, and on the "Home Show," "Geraldo," "Today Show," "Larry King Live," and "CBS This Morning" TV shows. ACES has also been featured in the Ann Landers newspaper column, *Working Mother* magazine, National Public Radio's "All Things Considered," Associated Press and United Press International articles, and in various local newspapers, TV, and radio features.

ACES has provided workshops for Employer Associations, The Displaced Homemaker Associations, Organization For the Education of Young Children, and the National Headstart Conference in 1987.

Geraldine Jensen, president of ACES is a member of the U.S. Commission on Interstate Child Support, and was given the Citizen's Award for "Child Advocacy" by the Ohio

Organization for the Education for Young Children, received a national award for child support "Program Awareness" from the National Association for Child Support Enforcement in 1987, the Jefferson Award in 1988, Ohio Women's Hall of Fame in 1989, and National Organization of Women's Education and Legal Defense Fund Award in 1989.

ACES was founded in Toledo, Ohio in March of 1984. In the past five years ACES has assisted over 70,000 children to receive child support payments to which they were entitled. These children's standard of living was increased on the average of $3,000 to $4,000 per year. The typical ACES client/member is a single female head of household with two children. She earns $8,906 per year and is owed $5,000 in back child support. Her family has subsisted at least in part on government benefits due to non-support.

ACES is dedicated to assisting disadvantaged children affected by parents who fail to meet child support/visitation obligations. It is the largest child support/visitation advocacy organization in the U.S., with almost 200 chapters in 46 states. The list of chapters is constantly changing and growing.

Please send a self-addressed stamped envelope to the ACES national office for a complete list.

ACES CHAPTERS ARE LOCATED IN THE FOLLOWING STATES

Alabama • Alaska • Arizona • Arkansas • California • Colorado • Connecticut • Delaware • District of Columbia • Florida • Georgia • Idaho • Illinois • Indiana • Iowa • Kansas • Kentucky • Louisiana • Maine • Maryland • Massachusetts • Michigan • Minnesota • Mississippi • Missouri • Montana • Nebraska • Nevada • New Jersey • New Mexico • New York • North Carolina • North Dakota • Ohio • Oklahoma • Oregon • Pennsylvania • South Carolina • Tennessee • Texas • Utah • Virginia • Washington • West Virginia • Wisconsin

For information to establish a chapter in your county, contact:

ACES
723 Phillips Avenue, Suite 216
Toledo, Ohio 43612
(419) 476–2511 or
1-(800)-537–7072

Contact the national office above for chapter phone numbers and addresses.

ACES Membership Application

See special membership offer that includes book
and reporting non-payor to Credit Bureau. ★★★★

Name _____

Address _____

City _____ County _____

State _____ Zip _____ Phone _____

_____ Membership dues enclosed ($18 per year)

_____ I would like to join ACES but cannot afford dues at
this time

_____ Reporting Non-Payor to TRW Credit Bureau ($15
members, $20 non-members)

_____ New Member with book ($24.50)

_____ ★★★★New Member Special Offer with book and reporting non-payor to Credit Bureau (Fill out TRW
Credit Bureau Form) ($29.95)

I understand that ACES does not guarantee receipt of child
support. ACES will provide members with information concerning their legal rights and remedies regarding child support
and visitation. Membership entitles you to receive the semi-
annual newsletter, reduced registration fees for conferences
and all other membership privileges.

Signature _____

Total enclosed _____

Please make checks payable to:
ACES
723 Phillips Ave., Suite 216, Toledo, OH 43612

Appendix B

Government Child Support Enforcement Offices (IV–D)

ALABAMA
Director
Bureau of Child Support
Department of Human Resources
50 Ripley
Montgomery, AL 36130
(205) 242–9300

ALASKA
Director
Child Support Enforcement Div.
Department of Revenue
550 West 7th Avenue, 4th Floor
Anchorage, AK
(907) 276–3441

ARIZONA
Administrator
Child Support Enforcement Admin.
Department of Economic Security
P.O. Box 6123/Site Code 776-A
2222 W. Encanto
Phoenix, AZ 85005
(602) 252–0236

ARKANSAS
Director
Office of Child Support Enforcement
Arkansas Social Services
P.O. Box 3358
Little Rock, AR 72203
(501) 682–8398

CALIFORNIA
Chief
Child Support Program
Department of Social Services
744 P Street/Mail Stop 9–011
Sacramento, CA 95814
(916) 323–8994

COLORADO
Director
Division of Child Support
Department of Social Services
1575 Sherman
Denver, CO 80203–1714
(303) 866–5994

CONNECTICUT
Director
Bureau of Child Support Enforcement
Dept of Human Resources
1049 Asylum Avenue
Hartford, CT 06105
(203) 566–3053

DELAWARE
Director
Division of Child Support
Department of Health & Social Srvs.
P.O. Box 904
New Castle, DE 19720
(302) 421–8300

DISTRICT OF COLUMBIA
Chief
Office of Paternity & Child Support
Department of Human Services
425 "I" Street, N.W. 3rd Floor
Washington, D.C. 20001
(202) 724–5610

FLORIDA
Director
Office of Child Support Enforcement
Dept. of Health & Rehabilitative
1317 Winewood Blvd. Bldg-3
Tallahassee, FL 32399–0700
(904) 488-9900

GEORGIA
Director
Office of Child Support Recovery
State Dept. of Human Resources
878 Peach Tree N.E.
Atlanta, GA 30309
(404) 894–4119

GUAM
Asst. District Attny.
Office of the Attorney General
Union Bank
194 Hernan Cortez Avenue
Agana, Guam 96910
(671) 477–2036

HAWAII
Director
Child Support Enforcement Agency
Department of Attorney General
Box 1860
Honolulu, HI 96805
(808) 587–3712

IDAHO
Chief
Bureau of Child Support Enforcement
Department of Health & Welfare
450 W. State Street, 7th Floor
Towers Building
Boise, ID 83720
(208) 334–5710

ILLINOIS
Chief
Bureau of Child Support Enforcement
Illinois Department of Public Aid

Bloom Building
P.O. Box 19405, 20L S. Grand Ave.
E.
Springfield, IL 82705
(217) 782–1366

INDIANA
Director
Child Support Enforcement Division
Department of Public Welfare
141 South Meridan, 4th Floor
Indianapolis, IN 46225
(317) 232–4885

IOWA
Chief
Bureau of Collections
Iowa Department of Human Services
Hoover Building - 5th Floor
Des Moines, IA 50319
(515) 281–5580

KANSAS
Administrator
Child Support Enforcement Program
Dept. of Social & Rehabilitation Srv.
300 S.W. Okaley St., Biddle Building
P.O. Box 497
Topeka, KS 66603
(913) 296–3237

LOUISIANA
Director
Support Enforcement Services
Department of Social Services
P.O. Box 94065
Baton Rouge, LA 70804
(504) 342–4780

MAINE
Director
Support Enforcement and Location
Bureau of Social Welfare
Department of Human Services
State House, Station 11
Augusta, ME 04333
(207) 289–2886

MARYLAND
Executive Director
Child Support Enforcement Admin.
Department of Human Resources
311 W. Saratoga, 3rd Floor
Baltimore, MD 31201
(301) 333–3978

MASSACHUSETTS
Deputy Commissioner
Child Support Enforcement Unit
Department of Revenue
141 Portland
Cambridge, MA 02139
(617) 727–3950

MICHIGAN
Director
Office of Child Support
Department of Social Services
235 Grand Avenue #L406
P.O. Box 30037
Lansing, MI 48909
(517) 373–7570

MINNESOTA
Director
Office of Child Support
Department of Human Services
444 Lafayette, 4th Floor
St. Paul, MN 55155
(612) 296–2499

KENTUCKY
Director
Division of Child Support Enforcement
Department of Social Insurance
Cabinet for Human Resources
725 East Main Street, 6th Floor East
Frankfort, KY 40621
(502) 564–2285

MISSISSIPPI
Director
Child Support Division
State Department of Public Welfare
P.O. Box 352, 515 E. Amite Street
Jackson, MS 39205
(601) 354–0341, Ext. 503

MISSOURI
Administrator
Child Support Enforcement Unit
Division of Legal Services
Dept. Of Social Services
P.O. Box 1527
Jefferson City, MO 65102–1527
(314) 751–4301

MONTANA
Director
Child Support Enforcement Program
Department of Social & Rehab. Srvc.
P.O. Box 5955
Helena, MT 59604
(406) 444–4614

NEBRASKA
Administrator
Child Support Enforcement Office
Department of Social Services
P.O. Box 95026
Lincoln, NE 68509
(402) 471–9125

NEVADA
Director
Child Support Enforcement Program
Department of Human Resources
2527 N. Carson Street
Services
Capital Complex
Carson City, NV 89710
(702) 885–4744

NEW JERSEY
Director
New Jersey Div. of Public Welfare
Bureau of Child Support & Paternity
CN 715
Trenton, NJ 08625
(609) 588–2401

NEW MEXICO
Chief
Child Support Enforcement Bureau
Department of Human Services
P.O. Box 25109
Santa Fe, NM 87503
(505) 827–4230

NEW YORK
Director
Office of Child Support Enforcement
New York State Dept. of Social Srvs
P.O. Box 14
1 Commerce Plaza
Albany, NY 12280
(518) 474–9081

NORTH CAROLINA
Chief
Child Support Enforcement Section
Division of Social Services
Depart of Human Resources
100 E. Six Forks
Raleigh, NC 27609
(919) 571–4120

NORTH DAKOTA
Administrator
Child Support Enforcement Agency
North Dakota Dept. of Human
State Capital
Bismarck, ND 58505
(701) 224–3582

NEW HAMPSHIRE
Administrator
Office of Child Support Enfor. Srvs.
Division of Welfare
Health & Welfare Building
6 Hazen Drive
Concord, NH 03301
(603) 271–4426

OKLAHOMA
Administrator
Division of Child Support
Department of Human Services
P.O. Box 25352
Oklahoma City, OK 73125
(405) 424–5871

OREGON
Director
Recovery Services Section
Adult and Family Services Div.
Department of Human Resources
P.O. Box 14506
Salem, OR 97309
(503) 378–5439

PENNSYLVANIA
Director
Child Support Programs
Bureau of Claim Settlement
P.O. Box 8018
Harrisburg, PA 17105
(717) 783–8729

PUERTO RICO
Director
Child Support Enforcement Program
Department of Social Services
CALL Box 3349
San Juan, PR 00904
(809) 722–4731

RHODE ISLAND
Chief Supervisor
Bureau of Family Support
Department of Social & Rehab. Srvs.
77 Dorance Street
Providence, RI 02903
(401) 277–2409

OHIO
Chief
Bureau of Child Support
Ohio Dept. of Human Services
State Office Tower
30 East Broad Street-27th Floor
Columbus, OH 43266–0423
(614) 466–3233

SOUTH DAKOTA
Program Administrator
Office of Child Support Enforcement
Depart of Social Services
700 Governors Drive
Pierre, SD 57501–2291
(605) 773–3641

TENNESSEE
Director
Child Support Services
Department of Human Services
Citizens Plaza Bldg. 12th Floor
400 Deadrick Street
Nashville, TN 37219
(615) 741–1820

TEXAS
Director
Child Support Enforcement Division
c/o Attorney General's Office
P.O. Box 12548
Austin, TX 78711–2017
(512) 463–2181

UTAH
Director
Office of Recovery Services
Department of Social Services
120 N. 200 West/P.O. Box 45011
Salt Lake City, UT 84145–0011
(801) 538–4400

VERMONT
Director
Child Support Division
Department of Social Welfare
103 South Main Street
Waterbury, VT 05676
(802) 241–2319

SOUTH CAROLINA
Director
Child Support Enforcement Division
Department of Social Services
P.O. Box 1520
Columbia, SC 29202–9988
(803) 737–9938

VIRGINIA
Director
Division of Support Enforcement
Department of Social Services
8007 Discovery Drive
Richmond, VA 23288
(804) 662–9629

WASHINGTON
Chief
Office of Support Enforcement

Revenue Division
Department of Social & Health Srvs
Mailstop HJ-31
Olympia, WA 98504
(206) 459–6481

WEST VIRGINIA
Director
Office of Child Support Enforcement
Department of Human Services
State Capitol Complex
Building #6, Room 812
Charleston, WV 25305
(304) 348–3780

VIRGIN ISLANDS
Director
Support and Paternity Division
Department of Justice
48B-50C Kronprindsens Gade
GERS Complex - 2nd Floor
St. Thomas, VI 00802
(809) 776–0372

WISCONSIN
Director
Division of Community Services
Office of Child Support
1 West Wilson Street, Room 382
P.O. Box 7935
Madison, WI 53707–7935
(608) 266–9909

WYOMING
Director
Child Support Enforcement Section
Div. of Public Asst. & Social Srvs.
State Dept. of Health & Social Srv.
Hathaway Building
Cheyenne, WY 82002
(307) 777–7892

Rev. 5/91

REGIONAL OFFICES OF THE
OFFICE OF CHILD SUPPORT ENFORCEMENT

REGION I—Connecticut, Maine, Massachusetts, New Hampshire, Rhode Island, Vermont
OCSE Regional Representative
John F. Kennedy Federal Building, Room 1500
Government Center
Boston, MA 02203
(617) 565–2475

REGION II—New York, New Jersey, Puerto Rico, Virgin Islands
OCSE Regional Representative
Federal Building, Room 4048
26 Federal Plaza
New York, NY 10278
(212) 264–7170

REGION III—Delaware, Maryland, Pennsylvania, Virginia, West Virginia, District of Columbia
OCSE Regional Representative
P.O. Box 8436
3535 Market Street, Room 5220
Philadelphia, PA 19101
(215) 596–1320

REGION IV—Alabama, Florida, Georgia, Kentucky, Mississippi, North Carolina, South Carolina, Tennessee
OCSE Regional Representative
101 Marietta Tower, Suite 821
Atlanta, GA 30323
(404) 331–2180

REGION V—Illinois, Indiana, Michigan, Minnesota, Ohio, Wisconsin
OCSE Regional Representative
105 W. Adams St., 20th Floor
Chicago, IL 60606
(312) 353–4237

REGION VI—Arkansas, Louisiana, New Mexico, Oklahoma, Texas
OCSE Regional Representative
1200 Main Tower Building, Suite 1700
Dallas, TX 75202
(214) 767–4155

REGION VII—Iowa, Kansas, Missouri, Nebraska
OCSE Regional Representative
601 East 12th Street
Federal Building, Room 515
Kansas City, MO 64106
(816) 426–5981

REGION VIII—Colorado, Montana, North Dakota, South Dakota, Utah, Wyoming
OCSE Regional Representative
Federal Office Building, Room 1185
1961 Stout Street
Denver, CO 80294
(303) 844–5594

REGION IX—Arizona, California, Hawaii, Nevada, Guam
OCSE Regional Representative
50 United Nations Plaza, Mail Stop 351
San Francisco, CA 94102
(415) 556–5176

REGION X—Alaska, Idaho, Oregon, Washington
OCSE Regional Representative
Third and Broad Building
2901 Third Avenue, Mail Stop 305
Seattle, WA 98121
(206) 553–2430

Appendix C
Legal Rights
NEW CHILD SUPPORT TIMEFRAMES-NEW LEGAL
RIGHTS FOR YOU!

ON OCTOBER 1, 1990 IT IS **TIME** for action for Child
Support Enforcement in the United States. New federal
timeframes for Child Support go into effect. These timeframes are designed to ensure faster and better action to
collect child support. **These laws are effective in your state
on October 1, too!**
Government Child Support Agencies will now have to
follow these 10 new rules:

1. Open cases within 20 day of families applying for help.
   Case opening includes immediately giving you an application if
   you personally go to the agency and request it; mail one to you
   within five days if you call on the phone or write them asking
   for an application. **Decide what action needs to be taken on
   your case such as;** location of the non-payor, or starting a
   process to do a payroll deduction, etc.
2. Attempt to locate absent parents within 75 days and repeat
   location attempts quarterly.
   Location includes a federal parent locator if no address is known
   anywhere in the U.S. This includes checking Social Security
   records, IRS records, V.A. records, etc. A state parent locator if
   the state where the non-payor lives is known but no specific
   street address or employer address is known. State parent
   locator includes checking State Department of Motor Vehicles,
   State Employment Bureau Records, State Workers' Compensation records, Welfare records, tax records, etc. **Location is
   defined as physical whereabouts and source of income/as-
   sets.**

3. Begin legal process to establish paternity within 90 days of locating the absent parent.
   The establishing paternity 90-day timeframe begins the day after the alleged father is located if necessary. Paternity is a legal process where a certain man is legally proven to be the father of a certain child. If the alleged father denies paternity, courts must order blood tests which are genetically based to determine if the man is the child's father.

4. Establish a court order within 90 days of locating the absent parent.
   The timeframe for establishing a court order begins the day after the non-payor is located if this is necessary. This process is needed if you have been deserted or are separated from the child's father. The court order sets up an amount of support to be paid.

5. Identify cases where no payment has been made for one month, automatically initiate action to collect the support via payroll deduction, and complete the action to collect the support within 60 days.
   This law adds timeframes to current law provisions.

6. Monitor cases to ensure health insurance coverage for the children is in place, and take action to enforce health care insurance if it lapses.
   This is a **NEW** law and the child support agencies must monitor cases for the first time. Previously they had to take action to enforce medical support and establish orders but only if the family entitled to the support complained.

7. Submit all cases each year to the IRS for attachment of federal income tax refunds. If $500.00 in back support is owed for non-welfare families, or $150.00 is owed in back support for welfare families.
   Previously the child support agency could 'pick and choose' which cases to submit.

8. Distribute support payments collected to families within 15 days of receipt.
   Distributing payments includes the following special rules:
   - If you are on welfare and more than $50.00 is paid, you receive the first $50.00 paid within 15 days after the payment is received by the Welfare agency from the Child Support Agency. The child support agency has 10 days to send the payment to the Welfare Department.
   - If you are not on Welfare, the government must send the payment to you within 15 days even in states where payments are paid to the clerk of courts who then sends the money to the State Agency handling the child support, who sends the payment to the family owed support.

- On out-of-state cases, each state gets 15 days to process the payments. You should receive the payment within 30 days after it is paid to the first state. Example: SD pays KY on Sept. 1, KY sends the payment to NY on Sept. 15. NY sends the payment to you by Sept. 30.

9. Make diligent efforts to serve legal notice to absent parents of hearings and document such efforts.

Sheriffs and process servers must try more than once to deliver notice of court hearing, payroll deductions, legal documents on the non-payor. If they cannot personally serve the papers and/or if they cannot serve the papers by certified mail, the sheriff, process server and/or child support agency must document efforts to serve the paper and prove to you they did indeed try several times.

10. Follow specific criteria to close cases, and notify the family owed support 60 days before a case is closed.

Specific reasons they may close a case include: 1. Child has reached age of majority, there is no longer a current order for support, and there is no arrearage, the arrearage is less than $500 or the order is unenforceable under state law; 2. Death of an absent parent, alleged father occurs and there is no further action that can be taken such as levy against the estate; 3. Child has reached age 18 and action to establish paternity is prohibited by state law or blood tests have excluded alleged father or alleged father cannot be identified. May also be closed if birth is a result of incest, rape or adoption is pending or a finding of a good cause by IV-A has been made; 4. If IV-D has been unable to locate absent parent after making repeated location attempts via state/federal parent locator over a three-year period; 5. If the absent parent is in jail, a psychiatric institution or has a verifiable medical total permanent disability with no evidence of support potential. The state must determine that there is no income or assets available to the absent parent which can be attached for support; 6. If the absent parent is a citizen of a foreign country, lives in the foreign country, does not work for the U.S. Government, or a U.S. company and has no U.S. source of income or assets and the state cannot get a reciprocal agreement with the country where the non-payor lives to collect support; 7. If the case was opened for location only services, it is closed once the location services have been provided; 8. If a non-AFDC client requests closure and there is no arrearage owed to the state; 9. If there has been a finding by the IV-A agency (Welfare Dept.) against the custodial parent for failure to cooperate: 10. If IV-D is unable to contact the custodial parent for at least 30 calendar days. Attempts must include phone, letter, and at least one registered letter.

CFR Section 303.11 requires states to notify families 60 calendar days prior to case closure in writing. The case may be left open if the custodial parent supplies information which gives the agency further leads to establish paternity, or a court order to enforce the support order or enforcement of an order. If IV-D agencies are required to keep cases on file after a closure for three (3) years.

SAMPLE:

Motion to Show Cause for Contempt of
Court of non-payment of Medical bills.

In The Common Pleas Court of Cuyahoga County, Ohio.

MARY SMITH   )   CASE #: DR60000
Plaintiff   )
)
        vs   )
)
)
JOHN SMITH   )
)   Motion to Show Cause
Defendant   )
)

Now come the plaintiff, Ms. Mary Smith and states that on
January 1, 1986 an order was entered in the above cause which
provides as follows: John Smith, defendant, was ordered* to pay
all medical expenses for children Sally Jo Smith and Mike Smith.

Plaintiff states that defendant has violated said order in that:
There are $359.00 of medical bills from St. Joseph's Hospital
which the defendant has not paid when requested to do so by the
plaintiff.

Wherefore, Plaintiff moves that defendant be cited to appear before the Court to show why he should not be punished for contempt
of Court.

                    _____

                              Signature

*Copy exactly as written in last Court Order (Journal Entry)

Pro Se

    1) Type your own motion; follow sample as a guide.

    2) Take to Clerk of Courts—and file. There will be a filing
       fee unless you also file a notarized statement which states
       you cannot afford the filing fee.

    3) Get Court date from assignment clerk. Should be able to
       tell you when you file motion.

Appendix D

How To Complain Effectively

If you have completed an application for assistance to collect child support at your local child support agency (4-D) and they have failed to assist you:

1. Write a short to-the-point letter about what action you need on your case. Send a copy of it to:
   a. Director of your local child support agency.
   b. The state child support agency where you live.
   c. The regional office of child support.
2. Wait 2 weeks. If no one has written back to you or called you: Call the regional office of child support for your state and call ACES. We can help you get action on your case—(419)476–2511.

SAMPLE COMPLAINT LETTER:

September 29, 1989

Dear Director:

On August 10, 1989, I requested Clark County Child Support Agency to locate my child's father. The agency has failed to take action on my case. Please advise me about what action is being taken on my case:

My name:	Mary Smith
Address:	1111 Oak St., Toledo, OH 43666
Phone:	(419)555–1111
Case Number:	

Non-payor name: John Smith
Social Security Number: (if known)
Last known address:

Sincerely,

Mary Smith

ACES Chapters help families owed support through "group complaints" and by providing you information about local agencies and your legal rights. Join a chapter, get involved. Call 1(800)537–7072 to locate a chapter near you.

Appendix E
Emergency Organizations

Most communities have an Information and Referral which can direct you to local social service agencies available to help you obtain emergency food, clothing and shelter.

Following is a list of those organizations.

Salvation Army/Volunteers of America/St. Vincent de Paul Society all have clothing and sometimes food. They often can refer you to the social service agency in the community that has emergency housing money available.

State Welfare Department (Department of Social Services, Human Resources, etc.) can provide food stamps, medical assistance (Medicaid) and cash assistance (Aid to Families with Dependent Children) for those meeting eligibility requirements.

Goodwill Industries has furniture, clothing and other household items.

Catholic Social Services in most communities throughout the U.S. can assist you with contacting a "Feed Your Neighbor" program, which has food and emergency cash assistance.

Child care assistance may be available to you for in-home or day care centers based on the number of children you have and your income through Title XX funds. Apply at your local welfare/social service agency. Usually, your income must be under $25,000.

You may be eligible for Medicaid based on your income, and special programs are available to single-parent families. Contact your local welfare department.

Community organizations and local churches have the people and resources available to help fix plumbing, furnaces and to do household repairs and refurbishing. Call them for referrals.

Traveler Aide has emergency shelter and cash to those who are stranded.

Planned Parenthood has low-cost or free birth control available.

Parents Without Partners offers a support group for single parents.

Lion's Club provides eye glasses for low-income families.

Big Brother/Big Sister provides an adult to fill the emotional gap left by an absent parent.

The Shriners help children in need of medical care.

American Red Cross provides social services to family members of the military and disaster victims.

Community Mental Health centers often change fees based on income for family counseling.

Home Energy Assistance Program (HEAP) provides assistance with utility bills.

Legal Aide/Legal Services provides low-income citizens with attorneys to handle legal matters. They might provide an attorney to handle a problem you are encountering with custody, visitation or domestic violence. Very few legal aides handle child support cases.

Domestic Violence/Battered Women's Shelters provide emergency shelter for those being physically abused by a family member or live-in.

Health Department offers free vaccines and immunizations to children.

For assistance with pre-natal health care, contact your state social service/welfare department. Assistance may be available in your area for low-income women.

The National Center for Missing and Exploited Children can be reached at 1-(800)–843–5678.

Parents Anonymous provides counseling services and advice for parents and others concerned about child abuse and neglect. They can be reached at 1 (800)–421–0353.

Hospitals are required by law to provide free or reduced charges for care to those who qualify because of low income. For Low Income Assistance/Hill Burton, call 1-(800)–638–0742.

Appendix F
After Your Divorce . . .

Here is a list of issues, some of which ACES recommends including as provisions of your court order to protect your children. These are very general; discuss each of them in depth with your attorney. If you are low-income, you can contact a Legal Aid Society or bar association "pro bono" program for free assistance.

1. *Custody:* sole custody—children's rights; parent's rights; joint custody—children's rights, parent's rights; guidelines for parents, schedule, legal residency, transportation.

2. *Visitation:* Children's rights, guidelines for parents, schedules, transportation, moves out of state by either parent.

If there are visitation disputes, a set schedule agreed to in the order will sometimes alleviate problems. The schedule should include days and times of visitation. It should also include provisions for special needs of the child, medical care, nutritional needs, and the child's activities such as Cub Scouts, sports, etc.

3. *Child support:* Method of payment—income withholding order to collect from those who are working and receive regular pay checks.

Posting of bond to ensure payments and automatic deduction from bank accounts for those who are self-employed or irregular workers.

Minimum set amount, or attachment of unemployment benefits, and orders to seek work for those unemployed. Or, include an attachment of worker's compensation, rents received, or other income if applicable; plus a bond to assure performance.

4. *Other support issues:* Cost of living increases, length of support obligation to continue to emancipation or through college or post-secondary education.

Amount of support to be paid should be based on the state child support guidelines. If not, is the reason that the support is higher or lower fair equitable?

Modification in the future for needs of child or change in circumstances should not be prohibited in the court order and can be listed to occur at regular automatic intervals, such as every two years.

5. *Medical and dental care of child.* Medical insurance should include provisions for:

a. Who is responsible to provide health and dental insurance?
b. Who and how is the insurance to be paid for?
c. Who is responsible for paying the deductible on medical and dental insurance?
d. Who is responsible for paying bills not covered by insurance?
e. How are they to be paid, and by when?
f. Who is responsible for medical and dental insurance when the child is over age of majority but still a dependent (in college, etc.)?

Provisions should be included in the order that the custodial parent has direct access to the health and dental insurance company to obtain needed claim forms, submit claims and obtain ID cards even if the non-custodial parent is the insured party.

6. *Life insurance:* Is it going to be provided for the child, by whom, and is the child going to be listed as a beneficiary on either parent's life insurance?

7. *Car insurance:* Who is responsible to provide for children when they are old enough to drive?

8. *Tax issues:* The IRS automatically allows the custodial parent to claim the child as an exemption unless the custodial parent signs a waiver giving the right of exemption to the non-custodial parent. Child support is non-taxable, alimony is taxable income.

Appendix G

GLOSSARY

Absent Parent: An individual who is absent from the home and is legally responsible for providing financial support for a dependant child.

Action: An ordinary proceeding in a court by which one party sues another.

Adjudication: The entry of a judgment or decree by a judge surrogate after submission of evidence by all parties to the action.

Administrative Agency: An agency of the sovereign power charged with administering particular legislation. Examples are state welfare and state IV-D agencies.

Administrative Determination of Support: A support obligation arrived at as a result of the administrative process.

Administrative Enforcement: Attachment and execution of a responsible parent's assets by a state administrative agency, in lieu of a court, pursuant to authorizing statues.

Administrative Process: A system set up in a state agency by statute for the purpose of adjudicating contested cases.

Affidavit: A written declaration or statement of fact, made voluntarily and confirmed by oath or affirmation of the party making it, taken before an officer authorized to administer oaths.

Agent: A person authorized by another to act for him or her; a substitute or a deputy, appointed by a person and given discretionary power to act in his or her behalf.

Allegation: The assertion, declaration or statement of a party to a case, made in pleading, setting out what is expected to be proved.

Appeal: The request of a party to a higher court to review the rulings made in a lower court for possible errors that would justify overruling the lower court's judgment and perhaps granting a new trial.

Arrearage: The total unpaid support obligation owed by an absent parent.

Burden of Proof: The necessity or duty of affirmatively proving a fact in dispute on an issue raised between the parties.

Case Law: Law established by judicial decision in individual cases.

Claim: To demand as one's own; to assert, state, or insist; an allegation made in an action at law.

Common Law: A body of law developed in England primarily from judicial decisions based on custom and precedent, unwritten in statute or code, and constituting the basis of the English legal system.

Complainant: Person who seeks to initiate court proceedings against another person. In a civil case, the complainant is the plaintiff; in a criminal case the complainant is the state.

Complaint: The formal written document in a court whereby the person initiating the action sets forth the names of the parties, the allegations, and the request for relief sought; the initial pleading.

Contemnor: A person who has committed contempt of court.

Counsel: Attorneys or attorneys for a party.

Default: The failure of a defendant to file an answer or appear in a civil case within the applicable time period after having been properly served with a summons and complaint.

Dependent: A person to whom a duty of support is owed.

Deposition: The gathering of written statements from witnesses which are made under oath but not at the court hearing, and to be used later at the trial.

Docket: A formal brief record of proceedings in court; minute entries in case files; the court calendar. Some courts refer to filing a paper with the court as docketing.

Due Process: The conduct of legal proceedings according to those rules and principles which have established in our system of law for the enforcement and protection of private rights. Its most essential elements are a court with proper jurisdiction over the subject matter and the defendant, notice to each party, the opportunity for each party to present evidence and to challenge the opposing party's evidence, orderly procedures, and a neutral and unbiased trier of fact who determines the facts and decides the issues only on the basis of the persuasiveness of relevant evidence properly admitted, and review of that determination by a higher authority. Due process is a safeguard against unreasonable, arbitrary and capricious decisions.

Equity: A system of law originating in the English Chancery Courts and comprising a settled and formal body of legal procedural rules and doctrines that supplement, aid or override statutory law.

Execution: Any remedy that effects enforcement of a civil money judgment by ordering a sheriff to seize and sell the judgment debtor's real or personal property.

Ex parte: (Latin) Done for, in behalf of; a judicial procedure instituted by one party, without notice to or participation by any adverse party.

IV-D Agency: A single and separate organizational unit in a state that has the responsibility for administering the State Plan for Child Support Enforcement under Title IV-D of the Social Security Act.

Garnishee: The person in possession of a judgment debtor's property upon whom a garnishment is served.

Garnishment: A legal proceeding whereby a judgment debtor's property, money or credit in the possession of or under the control of a third person (garnishee) is seized and applied in the payment of the judgment.

Hearing Officer: A referee authorized by state statute to preside over administrative hearings.

Initial Enforcement Techniques: Methods that may be used to convince an absent parent to pay child support without involving a court of law; usually accomplished by personal contact and persuasive arguments.

Interrogatories: Formal question(s) used to gather evidence.

Judgment: The official decision or legal finding upon the respective rights and claims of the parties to an action; also known as a decree or order and may include "findings of fact and conclusions of law."

Judicial Remedy: A mechanism for enforcement of court-imposed obligations. More specifically, any such mechanism imposed by a court, including contempt, execution, liens, bonds and other forms of security, garnishment, and involuntary wage assignment.

Judicial Review: A reconsideration or review by a court of a case tried in a lower court or administrative hearing; such review is usually restricted to material error and abuse of judicial discretion.

Jurisdiction: The express constitutional or legislative determination of what types of cases may be heard by certain courts. Before a court has jurisdiction, i.e., in order for the court to invoke its authority to try a case, the legislative criteria prescribing the class of cases which may be heard must be satisfied. These criteria encompass fixed geographical boundaries, the amount of money involved in a civil action, those parties who may lawfully be brought before the court, the types of civil claims which may be acted upon, and those criminal proceedings which may be conducted.

"Concurrent Jurisdiction": The authority of several different courts to deal with the same subject matter.

"Jurisdiction of the person": is the court's power to subject parties in a particular case to decisions and rulings made in the case.

"Subject-matter jurisdiction": means jurisdiction over the class of cases to which a particular case belongs.

"General Jurisdiction": Jurisdiction extending to all cases without any limitation as to subject matter.

"Limited jurisdiction": jurisdiction extending to only those classes of cases and proceedings specifically granted by statute. Common examples are courts with jurisdiction over all civil cases where the amount in controversy is less than a specified amount, or jurisdiction to try all misdemeanors but to conduct only preliminary hearings of felonies.

"Territorial jurisdiction": limits the court's authority to cases arising, or persons residing, within a defined territory such as a county or a judicial district.

Lien: A remedy that creates an encumbrance on the real or personal property of the judgment debtor.

Material Evidence: Important, having influence or effect; going to the substantial issues in dispute.

Motion: An application to a judge for an order or ruling.

Non-court ordered case: Cases in which no court has issued a support order.

Obligation: The legal amount of support owed for the benefit of children as ordered by a court or through administrative procedure.

Obligee: The person to whom a duty of support is owed.

Obligor: The person owing a duty of support.

Order: Any direction of a judge or hearing officer to a person, made or entered in writing, and not included in a judgment.

Plaintiff: A person who brings an action; the party who complains or sues in a civil case.

Pleadings: Written allegations filed with the court of what is affirmed on one side and denied on the other, disclosing to the court or jury the issue between the parties.

Pleading Practice: The process performed by the parties to an action by alternately presenting written statements of their contention. Each pleading is responsive to that which precedes it, and each serves to narrow the field of controversy until the evolvement of a single point, affirmed on one side and denied on the other (called an "issue") on which the parties then go to trial.

Precedent: An adjudged case or decision that serves as an example or authority for an identical or similar case or similar question of law.

Preponderance of the Evidence: Evidence with a superiority of persuasion. A judge cannot properly render verdict upon evidence in favor of the one having the burden of proof unless such evidence overbears, in some degree, the persuasiveness of the other side's evidence. This is the burden required in most civil cases. A higher standard is required of the prosecution in a criminal case.

Prima Facie Case: Evidence which is legally sufficient to establish a fact or case unless disproved.

Public Assistance: Support money or goods granted by a government entity to a person or family based on lack of income.

Real Property: Land or land-related property, such as houses and buildings.

Relevancy: Quality of evidence which bears directly on a fact in issue and tends to prove the existence or nonexistence of that fact.

Seizure: The taking of an object from its possessor or custodian by a law enforcement officer.

Service of Process: The delivery of a writ, summons, or other notice to the party to whom it is directed for the purpose of obtaining personal jurisdiction over that party.

Show Cause: A court order directing a person to appear and bring forth such evidence as one has, to offer reasons why the remedies state in the order should not be confirmed or executed. A show cause order is usually based on a motion and affidavit asking for relief.

Stipulation: An agreement between parties through their attorneys, if any, respecting business before the court. Most stipulations are required to be in writing.

Subpoena: An officer document ordering a person to appear in court or to bring and/or send documentation.

Substantive Law: Law that governs the rights, duties, and liabilities of the parties and defines the issues which the evidence must prove.

Summons: A notice to a defendant that an action against him or her has been commenced in the court issuing the summons and that a judgment will be taken against him or her if the complaint is not answered within a specified time.

Trial de novo: A new trial or retrial held in a higher court as if not trial had been held in a lower court.

Wage Assignment: A transfer, through automatic deductions from a persons wages, of money to pay a debt such as child support; the assignment may be voluntary or involuntary. In a voluntary assignment, the wage earner agrees to such a withholding. In an involuntary assignment, the court orders the wage earner to assign wages or suffer a contempt finding.

Withhold and Deliver: An administrative execution remedy, similar to garnishment, in which a third party is ordered to withhold property belonging to an obigor, and turn the property over to the plaintiff.

Writ: An order issuing from a court and requiring the performance of a specified act, or giving authority and permission to have it done.

Writ of Attachment: A court order employed to enforce obedience to an order or judgment of the court. (1) A warrant for the arrest of a person who is in contempt of court (body attachment or bench warrant); (2) A writ ordering the sheriff to seize the defendants' property in a civil case to prevent the defendant from hiding it or disposing of it before trial; and (3) A write of fieri facias.

Writ of Fieri Facias: (Latin) A court order directing a sheriff to seize money or personal property of a defendant to satisfy a money judgment held by the plaintiff. More commonly called a writ of execution.

GERALDINE JENSEN

Geraldine Jensen is the president and founder of the nationally recognized Association For Children For Enforcement Of Support (ACES), based in Toledo, Ohio. She has lectured across the country for associations, universities and has testified before the United States Congress. Through her personal experiences of having difficulty collecting child support, as well as her work with ACES, Ms. Jensen has been featured on "The Today Show," "CBS 48 Hours," "ABC Home Show," "Larry King Live" and "Geraldo," and has been written about in numerous Associated Press articles and national magazines.

Founded in 1984, ACES has grown to almost 20,000 members nationwide, with 200 chapters in 46 states.

Her activist work lead to an appointment by the Bush administration to the U.S. Commission on Interstate Child Support and being named to the Federal Child Support Advisory Committee. She has won many awards and lives with her two sons, Matt and Jake, in Toledo.

KATINA Z. JONES

Katina Z. Jones is the markets editor of *Writer's Digest* magazine, and has written for *McCall's, Crain's, Cleveland Business, Beacon Journal, Cincinnati Post* and several business and trade journals. Prior to becoming a full-time freelance writer, she was an award-winning editor of *Everybody's News*, Cincinnati's arts/entertainment bi-weekly. She lives in Fairlawn, Ohio with her husband, Louis Romestant.